estherpress

Books for Courageous Women

ESTHER PRESS VISION

Publishing diverse voices that encourage and equip women to walk courageously in the light of God's truth for such a time as this.

BIBLICAL STATEMENT OF PURPOSE

"For if you remain silent at this time, relief and deliverance for the Jews will arise from another place, but you and your father's family will perish. And who knows but that you have come to your royal position for such a time as this?"

– Esther 4:14

What people are saying about …

I Don't Even Like Women
And Other Lies That Get in the Way of Sacred Sisterhood

"I still remember how God answered me when I protested the call to minister to women, 'But, God, I don't like women!' Without any pause he replied, 'I do. I love women. I created woman as the answer to the very first problem. It was not good for the man to be alone.' And yet women often feel isolated in the company of one another. This needs to change. In her latest book, *I Don't Even Like Women*, Natalie challenges women of all ages to align with truth and stop repeating the lies. It is time to remember our why and build something beautiful and holy."

Lisa Bevere, *New York Times* bestselling author and cofounder of Messenger International

"I have known Natalie since she was in high school and have always appreciated her voice. She sees with her gift of discernment and says with her gift of mercy what the Church often needs to hear. I have such a heart for women, and for their role in kingdom advancement, and so it's with my whole heart I encourage you to consume *I Don't Even Like Women*. Ask the questions and take the risks that follow—your community will benefit and the Church will be strengthened."

Beth Guckenberger, author and speaker, Back2Back Ministries

"Natalie's poignant, humorous, and all-too-relatable words cut straight to the heart of what so many women have felt but rarely voiced. With authenticity and wisdom, she challenges the narratives that keep us divided and invites us into a deeper, sacred sisterhood. This book is a must-read for any woman longing for true connection and biblical community."

Jen Lilley, actress and producer

"I hope this book inspires us all to set aside pride, judgment, and past hurts, embracing instead the grace, compassion, and forgiveness that God freely gives to us as undeserving sinners. I admire Natalie's boldness in following God's prompting to write a book that will challenge and uplift many, just as it did for me."

Carly Patterson, Olympic gold medalist

"Natalie Runion does not mess around with this book. The healing and unity it offers women who have been wounded kicks Satan in the teeth and serves the body of Christ in a profound way. For every lie we've ever believed about each other, may the freedom words in these pages be our new song."

Lisa Whittle, bestselling author and Bible teacher

"You don't have to dislike women to relate to Natalie Runion's transformative words. In a world fixated on self-help and female empowerment, this book boldly calls us to step into the power already given to us through the Holy Spirit. Natalie reminds us that we don't have to fight for a seat at the table—it's already ours in Christ. She beautifully highlights how sacred sisterhood becomes possible when we let go of the petty lies we've believed about other women since high school. *I Don't Even Like Women* isn't a call to arms; it's a call to healing—a reminder that we don't have to prove ourselves, because in Christ, we are already enough."

Stephanie Gilbert, Jessica Taylor, and Jenna Allen of Pastors' Wives Tell All Podcast and Ministry, coauthors of *Pastors' Wives Tell All: Navigating Real Church Life with Honesty and Humor*

"Natalie doesn't just talk about sacred sisterhood—she lives it, writes it, and invites us into it. With grace, grit, and gut-level honesty, this book is a healing balm for every woman who's ever felt left out, let down, or like she doesn't belong. It will make you laugh, cry, and—most importantly—believe again in the beauty of God's design for friendship among women. You won't walk away the same."

Tammy Trent, author, speaker, singer, and cohost of *Life Today TV*

"When I first met Natalie, I felt like I'd known her my entire life. She just has that way about her—disarming your walls and making you feel instantly loved. That same warmth and authenticity shine through her writing. It's undeniable. As you turn the pages, you feel like you've found a lifelong friend. As a woman in ministry who has—regrettably—uttered the painful words *'I don't even like women,'* this book hit me straight to the core. It wasn't until Natalie gave space for this message that I realized I wasn't the only woman who had said those words—and truly meant them. What a gift it is to blow the dust off the cattiness and girl drama we've carried and uncover the tender sister, mother, daughter, and friend God created us to be. These pages are full of stinging truth and healing balm all at once. Natalie has a rare gift for offering both, and goodness, do we sisters need it. More than just endorse this book, I want to thank the author—our long-lost friend and sister—for writing it. Women, get ready. We need this."

Becky Johnson, lead pastor of Jesus Culture Sacramento

"I have had the honor of knowing Natalie her entire life; as cousins we were gifted with a solid Christian foundation. Our grandmother was a strong Christian woman who taught us that with God all things are possible, and our real treasures in life are found in seeking him first. How clear it can become that our true identity is not found in what we look like, in how much money we make, in how many times we get promoted ... rather in seeking, on a daily basis, to be more like Jesus, putting others before ourselves and watching God work miracles. I highly encourage you to embrace *I Don't Even Like*

Women, as it is very relevant and life-changing if we can dig deep into our own journey in life, asking the Holy Spirit to reveal all God has in store for us ... which is much greater than we can dream or imagine and all for the building of his Kingdom. Thank you, Natalie, for teaching us crucial lessons in how God wants us to navigate our time on earth. May we treasure each other, serving in the sisterhood to bring unity and glory to our Lord and Savior Jesus Christ."

Colleen Lindholz, president of Kroger Health

I Don't Even Like Women

USA Today Bestselling Author

Natalie Runion

I Don't Even Like Women

And Other Lies That Get in the Way of Sacred Sisterhood

150 YEARS STRONG
DAVID C COOK

I DON'T EVEN LIKE WOMEN
Published by Esther Press,
an imprint of David C Cook
4050 Lee Vance Drive
Colorado Springs, CO 80918 U.S.A.

Integrity Music Limited, a Division of David C Cook
Brighton, East Sussex BN1 2RE, England

DAVID C COOK®, the graphic circle C logo and related marks
are registered trademarks of David C Cook.

All rights reserved. Except for brief excerpts for review purposes,
no part of this book may be reproduced or used in any form
without written permission from the publisher.

The website addresses recommended throughout this book are offered as a resource
to you. These websites are not intended in any way to be or imply an endorsement
on the part of David C Cook, nor do we vouch for their content.

Details in some stories have been changed to protect the identities of the persons involved.

Unless otherwise noted, all Scripture quotations are taken from the Holy Bible, New Living Translation, copyright © 1996, 2015 by Tyndale House Foundation. Used by permission of Tyndale House Publishers, Carol Stream, Illinois 60188. All rights reserved. Scripture quotations marked NIV are taken from the Holy Bible, New International Version®, NIV®. Copyright © 1973, 2011 by Biblica, Inc.™ Used by permission of Zondervan. All rights reserved worldwide. www.zondervan.com. The "NIV" and "New International Version" are trademarks registered in the United States Patent and Trademark Office by Biblica, Inc.™; ESV are taken from the ESV® Bible (The Holy Bible, English Standard Version®), copyright © 2001 by Crossway, a publishing ministry of Good News Publishers. Used by permission. All rights reserved; and MSG are taken from THE MESSAGE, copyright © 1993, 2018 by Eugene H. Peterson. Used by permission of NavPress, represented by Tyndale House Publishers. All rights reserved. The author has added italics and boldface to Scripture quotations for emphasis.

Library of Congress Control Number 2025937007
ISBN 978-0-8307-8670-1
eISBN 978-0-8307-8673-2

© 2025 Natalie Ryan Runion
Published in association with the literary agency of WordServe
Literary Group, Ltd., www.wordserveliterary.com.

The Team: Susan McPherson, Stephanie Bennett, James Hershberger,
Jack Campbell, Michael Fedison, Susan Murdock
Cover Design: Brian Mellema
Cover Photos: Ashlee Kay Photography, http://ashleekay.com

Printed in the United States of America
First Edition 2025

1 2 3 4 5 6 7 8 9 10

*This one is for women everywhere.
My sacred sisters, my sister Stayers.
I don't just love you; I really like you.*

Contents

Introduction	17
Chapter 1: "I Don't Even Like Women ..."	27
Chapter 2: "Women Are So Mean ..."	43
Chapter 3: "Women Are Such Drama Queens ..."	59
Chapter 4: "Women Are So Insecure ..."	75
Chapter 5: "Women Are So Jealous ..."	91
Chapter 6: "Women Are So Emotional ..."	107
Chapter 7: "Women Are So Catty ..."	123
Chapter 8: "Women Are So Controlling ..."	141
Chapter 9: "Women Are So Competitive ..."	159
Chapter 10: "Women Belong in the ..."	177
Chapter 11: Golden Girls	197
Chapter 12: My Sister's Keeper	215
Epilogue	231
Notes	235

Introduction

I sit nervously in my supervisor's office, picking at my nails and scanning his beige walls as if the answer to why he has called this impromptu meeting might be found hiding behind his exquisitely framed college diplomas.

I have only been in my current position a little over a year, but this year has been tumultuous between girl drama on the team and other issues I can't seem to escape. As the moments tick on, I feel as if I am sitting in a hospital waiting room expecting to receive bad test results; I can't ignore the sick feeling in the pit of my stomach. Whatever we are meeting about must be urgent; otherwise, he would have saved it for our monthly one-on-one. Finally, I hear footsteps closing in, and as he walks across the threshold, he quietly closes his door behind him. I brace for impact.

"Natalie, I have called you in here today to let you know that church leadership would like to make a change in your role. You are a terrific worship leader and singer, but they feel you would be best suited in women's ministry ..."

His voice is now warbled and distorted to me, the room around me begins to spin, and heat rises from my chest to the tips of my ears. My blood pressure increases, and hot tears threaten to fall at any time.

It feels like my heart is now beating from within my head, and for maybe the second time in my life, I am at a complete loss for words. My eyes lift to his as he quietly waits for a reaction or a response.

"Natalie," he says with hesitation, "this is a promotion."

I know my response should be gracious, kind, full of gratitude, and perhaps ten years ago I would have responded in innocent glee. But age and experience—along with discernment—are throwing red flags up against these beige walls. All self-regulation and awareness flies out the window, and these words follow:

"WHAT?! WOMEN'S MINISTRY? ARE YOU KIDDING ME?

I DON'T EVEN LIKE WOMEN!"

Let's Back Up ...

It isn't that I don't like women—I do—but being a women's pastor in a local church was never on my bingo card. As a pastor's daughter I was a regular attendee alongside my mom and sister at women's ministry events involving fake flowers, bad tea parties, and foot-washing services where the women *kept their hose on*. I had spent my early twenties in the trenches of ministry first as a youth intern, then with children, and eventually worship leadership, and never once did thoughts of working exclusively with women cross my mind.

I have always preferred serving beside women and men. I enjoy sitting in meetings with both female and male perspectives, and to be clear, I have great respect for those called to pastor and lead large groups of women. But even as a child and teenager, my friend groups consisted mostly of guys. I attended a public high school in the '90s where mean girls ruled, skinny girls thrived, and I felt invisible. There were cliques and clichés, girl gangs and boss babes, and no matter how hard I tried to find my place among them, I never quite fit in. While my girlfriends in college rushed for sororities, I cheered them on from afar but was never interested in a perceived pseudo sisterhood that could easily sour.

It wasn't that I didn't like women.

I often felt rejected by women.

And in the local church, where sisterhood should be safe, I learned self-preservation as a life preserver. Public high school was child's play compared to what I would endure under the watchful eyes of women who would see me as their competition rather than their collaborator. My junior high cafeteria sectioned off by social class wasn't nearly as cutthroat as some of the women I would meet on the evangelical streets, each with their own versions of "you can't sit here" in attempts to keep queen bees in position and their hives under control.

My pastor's invitation to women's ministry felt more like an invitation to stepping on a hornet's nest without shoes, and it appeared I didn't have a choice.

Finding Honey

When it came time to design the cover art for my first book, I specifically asked my publisher not to use any pink or flowers on the cover. I wanted as much distance as possible from the stereotypical approach of other female authors often scripted on evangelical stages and online platforms for fear I'd be unfairly categorized or even canceled based on denominational assumptions, prejudice, and perception.

I myself had my own opinions and biases when it came to how women navigated their platforms and ministries. I didn't want to be known for my fashion choices or hairstyles. I didn't want to be branded simply because I was a wife and a mom or lose my unique voice in a noisy market of women trying to find their own voices.

It is also no secret that with time and maturity, women often "age out" of more visible areas of mainstream ministry and eventually find themselves funneled into women-centric roles that they might not choose but seem to be their only choice. The writing is on the wall: step into these opportunities with gratitude or go find another job.

I know I'm not the only woman who feels this way. Nearly every woman I meet who has found herself leading other women in any capacity, especially in women-focused ministry in churches around the world, has looked me in the eye and, in some variation, said, *"Trust me, I don't know how I got here. **I don't even like women.**"*

I know I can't speak for all women; I suppose there are the rare unicorns who have only known women to be kind, loving,

Introduction

and supportive throughout their lives. But it is my assumption that most of us who have lived on earth past puberty have had a few run-ins with fellow females that have left us a little baffled. It only takes one or two of these interactions to cause us to build walls to protect ourselves from getting hurt.

When I told friends and family I was writing this book, even those who worked for corporations found the topic intriguing, their husbands knowingly jabbing them in the side with an elbow and saying with a smile, "You need to read that." When I told women in the church—from the platform to the pew—that I was writing a book with this title, they started laughing, throwing their heads back and clapping their hands in delight. "Oh my gosh, haven't we said this very thing?!"

> **There is a hunger among women both inside and outside of church walls for authentic, pure friendship that, when tested, can be trusted.**

Their words feel like a confession, an apology mixed with a disclaimer, followed by what they are trying to do differently in their attempt to rewrite the script. But I am encouraged by their determination to challenge traditions and the cultures of their local churches to meet other women where they are in life and provide opportunities for biblical community in their grocery stores, kids' schools, gyms, and coffee shops. There is a hunger among women both inside and outside of church walls for authentic, pure friendship that, when tested, can be trusted.

But it isn't just this one statement, "I don't even like women," that has prompted me to write this book. Hundreds of other things I've thought or said out loud—or heard whispered by women—brought me to write these pages.

> *"Girls are mean."*
> *"Girls are so silly."*
> *"Teenage girls are dramatic."*
> *"Just wait until your daughter becomes a teen ..."*
> *"Women can be so petty."*
> *"She'd be so much prettier without all that work done."*
> *"I wonder how she got that position."*

We echo these quick quips without pause, perhaps under our breath in a sigh in a coffee shop while sitting across from a friend over morning lattes.

I have to ask myself, and now you, sacred sister: Do we actually believe these things, or have they become running scripts in our brains that we didn't write, but were written for us and we now simply repeat?

I believe that as women we want to like other women, but we're just so tired of feeling excluded by them or fighting them for a seat at a table. We long for friendship and deep conversation, but seasons of life, past experiences, and culture often keep us at arm's length from one another, sometimes to protect our hearts and other times because we simply don't have capacity for another relationship to maintain.

How do I know this? Because every time I conclude a women's conference with an invitation to come forward for prayer, one woman wraps her arms around another woman with almost always the same result: tears, relief, comfort, and belonging.

We have said out loud we don't like women, or we would rather be friends with men for various reasons, but it is my hope that together we will realize it simply isn't true. I pray that in the pages to come we rediscover our deep desire for biblical sisterhood that changes the way we think of and speak about one another and write a new script.

What I have learned in my own pursuit of sacred sisterhood: We will be stung a few times in our attempt to get to the honey, but the sweetness is worth the sting.

Pulling Out the Stinger

I'll never forget my supervisor's face as I impulsively confessed my disdain for women's ministry. I surprised myself at such honesty after years of people-pleasing and saying what I thought people wanted to hear to get out of awkward situations. But now my honest words were hanging in the air, and they couldn't be taken back. My reality was simple yet at the time tragic to me: step into this new role or have no role at all, and I loved the church too much to quit just because I wouldn't be leading worship.

So, I packed up my office and moved into a new space. My piano keyboard was replaced with comfy chairs where women would eventually sit and weep over failing marriages or prodigal children. I once practiced songs and memorized chord charts but would now prepare sermons and memorize scriptures. I once spent my days with musicians, but I would now sit in hospitals mourning with women who lost babies, officiate funerals of those I led, celebrate new engagements, and host breakfasts for women as I stepped up to lead a Bible study for the first time.

As these women learned to trust me as their leader and I grew to know their stories and families, I found I really did like women. God began to break my heart for his daughters because he really likes women.

He doesn't just like us. He adores us, loves us, cherishes us, and celebrates us.

Female friendships and relationships are hard, and nobody is harder on women than women. We are not only our own worst critics, but in our attempts to feel better about ourselves, we can pull each other down competing and comparing rather than collaborating.

This book isn't my attempt to call us into one giant slumber party of braiding each other's hair and telling deep, dark secrets, but rather is an invitation to be our sister's keeper.

To lead and love each other with respect, honor, and the knowledge that what God has placed inside a friend, neighbor, coworker, or sister isn't in competition with what he has placed inside us.

To speak of each other with highest regard and to pray for one another as if we were flesh and blood.

Introduction

To carry each other to the honey that can be found when women come together to contend for and celebrate one another even when our seasons aren't aligned or situations ideal.

To build tables so big we have to pull up more chairs because of all the room for our sisters.

To form a Kingdom army, not exclusive sororities.

To shift atmosphere rather than create silos.

To not just love each other, but to like each other.

The enemy is hoping we never figure out the authority we have in Christ as his unified daughters, because we are truly a force to be reckoned with, sisters.

> **The enemy is hoping we never figure out the authority we have in Christ as his unified daughters.**

So, let's get rid of the queen bees and get to work harvesting a honey that will sweeten even those most sour souls looking for sacred sisterhood. We will have to break down some lies, confront some stereotypes driven by mainstream media (and our own biases), and deal with our need for popularity and acceptance, but I think we're up to the challenge.

I need you.

I already love you.

And I really like you,

Natalie

Chapter 1

"I Don't Even Like Women ..."

and other things I've said in search of sacred sisterhood.

I am standing in the doorway, digging my toe into the carpet like a little girl showing up for her first day of school. My stomach is queasy despite the familiarity of many of the faces and the overplayed worship music filtering into the room, a looping soundtrack for the women who arrived thirty minutes early for the weekly gathering. They are dressed like typical Colorado women: layered neutrals on top, puffy vests or Patagonia down coats, but all business in boots on the bottom lest a spring snow fall in the next two hours and they should need to shovel themselves out of the church parking lot.

I had been leading these women in worship to start their Tuesday morning and Wednesday evening Bible studies for a year now. Part of my job description as a full-time worship pastor, in addition to leading worship for our Sunday morning services, was building a team made up primarily of volunteer female musicians and singers to staff the very busy women's ministry season.

Last year, I sent an email out to every woman who had expressed interest in the worship department in the past, as well as high-level volunteers who were on the weekly rotation, inviting them to a very early Saturday morning breakfast at the local IHOP restaurant. I figured anyone who showed up at 8:00 a.m. on a Saturday morning was probably serious about getting more information. But I braced myself for a breakfast for two—my eight-year-old daughter in tow who was only there for the funny-face pancakes.

When we arrived at the restaurant, the hostess told me there were already a few women waiting and walked me into the back room, where I found a group already gathered around tables they had pulled together. I began to introduce myself as others slowly trickled in, and before I knew it there were nearly thirty women elbow to elbow, forks clinking and syrup flowing, as I presented the opportunity to make some of their dreams of being part of an all-girl band come true.

There was a drummer in her mid-fifties working on her master's in theology. A few stay-at-home moms breastfeeding at the table played multiple instruments. A single girl in her twenties played the acoustic guitar like the '90s musician Jewel. That first year we spent hours together in rehearsals and worship services and slowly added to our roster as women showed up, scared but willing to serve.

I am now proud of what God has built among us in such a short amount of time. A weekly team of five women (plus an occasional brother from time to time) felt manageable. But leading hundreds of them at one time surrounded by fake flowers, miniature desserts, and the stereotypical female games like "What's in Your Purse?" to win silly prizes feels overwhelmingly exhausting.

I snap out of my daydream as the band begins to play, signaling to the women—and now to me as the new associate women's pastor—that it is time to begin. I'm sad I'm not with them behind the keyboard as I had been all the months before, angry I'm forced into this new role without any say in the matter.

The room is full now, and I've never felt more alone.

Everyone stands to worship, and several ladies turn to see where I am standing. I quickly smile through my tears to reassure them, I'm fine.

As I watch my friends on the platform, the tears can no longer be contained, so I let them fall, and as they sing, I'm writing my resignation letter in my head.

"To whom it may concern ..."

Where It All Began

I suppose we should go back many years to truly understand how I ended up in this position. The search for sacred sisterhood began long before elementary school, except it wasn't my search; rather, it was a mother's hope that her daughter would be blessed with a lifetime of sacred sisterhood. I don't know when this search began to be exact, but the faded Polaroid pictures stuck between pages of

> It was a mother's hope that her daughter would be blessed with a lifetime of sacred sisterhood.

vintage photo albums stored in my basement portray the universal yearning of my mom. I'm assuming all moms ...

There you will find me as a baby lying beside my newborn bestie in matching footy pj's, both purposefully donned in pink as our mothers, who had been childhood friends, posed us with hopes we would one day share this photo at our weddings, where we would stand beside one another as maids of honor.

There are pictures at ballet recitals where I'm squeezing the neck of another sequin-clad friend, blush-soaked cheeks pressed up against one another, our baby teeth hanging on for dear life as we cheesed it up for our proud parents. Dance friends for life, am I right?

You'll see me at Girl Scout Camp making friendship bracelets with my first-grade bestie, or at vacation Bible school with the new girl I met in the registration line when my mom told me, "Looks about your age." At the junior high dances in groups of adolescent glory, braces shining like diamonds on our big-girl teeth with knobby knees awkwardly posed inward to hide our emerging figures.

From an early age we were taught to look for one another in all seasons of life, to search for those sharing common interests and passions so we didn't have to do them alone. After all, isn't life better with a friend to live it beside you? Isn't that what every girl wants? And if it isn't, shouldn't it be?

Not long ago, while vacationing in Hawaii, my youngest daughter begged her older sister to join her in the frigid temperatures of the hotel pool. Bright-pink goggles glued to her face, she bobbed up and down, a little tanned buoy scanning the waters for anyone who might join her in a game of sharks and minnows.

Suddenly, a little girl in a neon-green face mask came to the surface and I watched in amazement as they locked eyes, complete strangers with a common goal: swimming their little hearts out until their lips turned blue. For the next three hours they didn't leave the water. Nobody had to make awkward introductions; the parents could take no credit for this newfound friendship. These two eleven-year-old little girls found one another all on their own, and by the end of the day, we were exchanging contact information as they stood side by side, huddled in beach towels, making plans for the rest of their time on the island.

Sure enough, at 9:00 a.m. the next day, as we walked out onto the sunny patio, we were met with "Selah!"—her new friend treading water in the deep end and waving her hand overhead. And for the remainder of the trip, her Hawaiian-vacation friend from South Dakota was a gift for a little girl who just wanted to play.

Created for Friendship

It sounds so simple, right? If eleven-year-old little girls can do it, surely by the time we reach adulthood we should be professionals at finding friendship. And not just finding it but keeping it and maintaining it with great care and precision.

From the very start of creation, God made humans with great purpose and intentionality. He wanted us to reflect his image, to occupy the earth, and to multiply. And he never intended for us to do it alone.

In creating Adam and Eve, he shows a clear desire to be in relationship with his creation, his children.

We were created for friendship.

Friendship with God.

Friendship with one another.

The fall of Adam and Eve would not only separate them from God and one another but carry generational consequences for future friendships and relationships between humankind. Two people created by God to see only the beauty in one another could now see every flaw and feel shame that was strong enough to cause them to hide from their Creator.

In addition to shame and embarrassment came selfish tactics to get what we wanted from one another. Adam may have felt manipulated when he realized Eve seemingly lured him into taking a bite of the fruit from the forbidden tree. Because of this decision, sin became part of our DNA. Humanity would continue to fall short of God's design for us—holiness, consecration, and sanctification—permanently separating us from our Creator physically and spiritually, and one another emotionally.

When I hear women say, "I don't even like women," which I myself have said on more than one occasion, I realize we're saying so much more. As fallen descendants of Eve, we are standing behind our tree, feeling exposed and rejected, afraid and insecure, revealing an honest cry of our heart:

> "I've never had a real friend..."
> "I've always wanted a sister..."
> "The last time I trusted another female I was hurt."
> "You have no idea the betrayal I watched my mom endure."
> "I feel inadequate and insecure when I'm around successful women."
> "I feel ugly and unseen when I think other girls are prettier than me."

When our little girls found swimming soulmates for that short week in Hawaii, their love for swimming with a friend overcame their fear of rejection. What they found in each other was someone to enjoy a moment of life with. That simplicity of friendship, the hope, can draw us out from behind the tree and back into the garden in search of sacred sisterhood, even when we want to hide.

Our Creator made us for fellowship with him and friendship with one another.

Women want friendship.

> **The simplicity of friendship, the hope, can draw us back into the garden in search of sacred sisterhood, even when we want to hide.**

Why does something that we seemingly want so badly feel nearly impossible as we grow from girlhood to womanhood?

I have to believe it's because the enemy of our soul wants us divided.

He knows when the daughters of God are united, when we stand confident and secure in our sacred sisterhood, we're a force to be reckoned with for the Kingdom of God.

Capitalizing off Caricature

Adding to our complex relational needs with the natural milestones unique to our upbringing, religion, and education, our culture, too, shapes our understanding of female friendships. Yet I find it interesting that even mainstream media has a difficult time creating a realistic image of healthy relationships between women. This results in a challenging Jenga-like structure that threatens to fall if one single piece is simply touched the wrong way with an opposing force. It's impossible to write a script that fully encompasses the nuances of female friendships. The heartbreaking reality is that sometimes we simply buy into simple stereotypes because it's too exhausting to work toward anything more—to write our own.

I believe that in the innocence of our youth, we as females truly desired pure, honest friendship. But at an early age we began believing the cultural narratives written for us, causing some of us to enter adolescence bracing for impact and others of us embracing the roles we perceive will provide power and popularity, allowing us to remain behind our tree while simultaneously ruling the garden.

After years of having these narratives forced upon us (and copying these narratives in our own lives), we often find ourselves discouraged when we realize we're isolated, lonely, and surrounded by shallow pseudo sisterhood. We think we've done everything right—looking like the girls in the movies or acting like the super popular girl in class that everyone adores—but something is missing.

Isn't this how I'm supposed to behave? Isn't this what gets me the boy? Isn't this what gets revenge? Isn't this how I win the war?

Current culture is confusing the roles of women in the world, in our relationships, and in how we engage with one another, affecting our impact in history and society. The messages are laced with a sinful worldview that's not at all aligned with the biblical blueprint we have been given where our Father reassures us of who we are and whose we are in his Word, calling us:

- CHOSEN—"Even before he made the world, God loved us and chose us in Christ to be holy and without fault in his eyes." (Eph. 1:4)
- LOVED—"And I am convinced that nothing can ever separate us from God's love. Neither death nor life, neither angels nor demons, neither our fears for today nor our worries about tomorrow—not even the powers of hell can separate us from God's love." (Rom. 8:38)
- FRIEND OF GOD—"I no longer call you slaves, because a master doesn't confide in

his slaves. Now you are my friends, since I have told you everything the Father told me." (John 15:15)
- ROOTED AND ESTABLISHED—"So that Christ may dwell in your hearts through faith—that you, being rooted and grounded in love, may have strength to comprehend with all the saints what is the breadth and length and height and depth, and to know the love of Christ that surpasses knowledge, that you may be filled with all the fullness of God." (Eph. 3:17–19 ESV)
- FEARFULLY AND WONDERFULLY MADE—"For you formed my inward parts; you knitted me together in my mother's womb. I praise you, for I am fearfully and wonderfully made. Wonderful are your works; my soul knows it very well." (Ps. 139:13–14 ESV)

Where the world magnifies the smallest flaws, amplifies the tiniest nuance, highlights every weakness, sweeps over an entire gender using microscopic generalizations with a broad brush, God speaks a better Word over us.

And he has the better plan for us.

I have good news for us, dear sisters. We don't have to hide, and we don't have to build a kingdom to rule. We can live the beautiful life God intended for us, together.

A Sacred Search

Sisters, God hears the desperate whispers in our hearts for friendship, and I like to think it is why he is so intentional in his Word to point us first toward our relationship with God—as we discovered in the garden—and then friendship with one another.

Observe the relationship between Elijah and Elisha in 2 Kings 2:2, where we are told Elijah wanted to ascend alone. "And Elijah said to Elisha, 'Stay here, for the LORD has told me to go to Bethel.' But Elisha replied, 'As surely as the LORD lives and you yourself live, I will never leave you!' So they went down **together** to Bethel."

We need friends who will witness the power and plan of God in our lives with their own eyes and not abandon us when the mission goes off course or gets dangerous.

Ecclesiastes 4:9–10: "Two people are better off than one, for they can help each other succeed. If one person falls, the other can reach out and help. But someone who falls alone is in real trouble."

Solomon is letting us know that even though we can do life alone, why would we if we don't have to? He is helping us understand the danger in solitude, for without another in our life we won't have that iron to sharpen us or to lead us away from sin when we stumble.

He goes on to say in verses 11–12, "Likewise, two people lying close together can keep each other warm. But how can one be warm alone? A person standing alone can be attacked and defeated, but two can stand back-to-back and conquer. Three are even better, for a triple-braided cord is not easily broken."

What a gift we have in friendship given to us from our good Father! We were meant to live this life across tables, not through the screens of our phones, online and isolated. Friendship offers us those who will fight with us and for us through prayer, words of encouragement, and even correction to protect us. Biblical friendship offers words of life in barren seasons and hope when all feels hopeless.

Biblical sisterhood is an invitation to community built on the Great Commandment of loving God and loving one another as Christ loves his Church, and that love is unconditional, free, and for us all.

Rewrite the Script

For those who have been on a lifetime search for friendship, it might feel far away and even unobtainable. It seems easy for others, but experiences and observations have led us to different conclusions.

You've believed you just get along better with males, that you're too loud or overbearing for other women, and that you like being an independent woman who doesn't need a sorority of sisters or gaggle of girls to make your life complete.

I used to believe all this myself, and I often find myself still fighting these lies. My hope in writing this book is that together we begin the tedious but sacred process of rewriting the script over this area of our lives.

Since the very beginning of creation, Satan has been trying to rewrite what God has already written. In Genesis chapter 3 verse 1 we are told, "Now the serpent was more crafty than any of the wild animals the LORD God had made. He said to the woman, 'Did God really say, "You must not eat from any tree in the garden"?'" (NIV).

This one question causes Eve to doubt what her loving Creator had spoken to her and Adam, instructions meant to protect them and keep them in fellowship with the one true God. Eve is able to recite the script of her Creator and responds to Satan, "We may eat fruit from the trees in the garden, but God did say, 'You must not eat fruit from the tree that is in the middle of the garden, and you must not touch it, or you will die'" (vv. 2–3 NIV).

Eve is confident in what she heard God say, but all it takes is one miniscule word reinterpretation in the script to change the entire plot. "'You will not certainly die,' the serpent said to the woman. 'For God knows that when you eat from it your eyes will be opened, and you will be like God, knowing good and evil'" (vv. 4–5 NIV).

It would be this one split second of believing a false narrative from the enemy of her soul that would not only change Adam and Eve's lives, but make them aware and ashamed of their nakedness, separating them from God.

Separating all men and women from God.

To redeem this separation, God sent his only Son, Jesus, to sacrifice himself. Jesus came to take on all our sin and shame to pay our debts so we can spend eternity with the One who created us for relationship with God—and one another. Satan may have tried to change the narrative, but God has always had the better script and now we have a choice: Do we allow Satan to change the narrative and give him control of the pen to our story, or do we stick to the script we know to be true, the Word of God?

It is my belief that, as women, we all want a friendship we will take with us to our graves. It is my prayer that in the pages ahead, you grab hold of hope and the promise that you are worthy and deserving of sacred sisterhood. So, let's rewrite a few of these false narratives and replace them with the gospel truth:

God loves women. God loves you.

And I pray by the end of our time together you will come out of hiding and be able to say to one another,

"I need you."

And maybe even,

"I like you."

Flip Your Script

It's important in allowing God to rewrite the script on sacred sisterhood that we take the next steps to flip the script in our own lives, living out a narrative that reflects the Father's heart for his daughters. Flipping the script is reflecting on our own lives as we confront a lifetime of lies written for us—and written by us—that have kept us from experiencing the joy of godly friendship with one another.

In the pages ahead we will end each chapter asking ourselves three key questions to help guide us on this journey to not only finding sacred sisterhood but toward healing, as some of our wounds might still be tender.

Let's practice this first one together.

1. **What lies have you believed about women that have gotten in the way of finding biblical, sacred sisterhood?**

2. **Was there a pivotal moment in your life where this became a script you adopted to protect your heart, or has it evolved over time?**

3. **Name a few obstacles or fears that make friendship difficult for you in this season of life. Maybe it's time, lack of community, fear of rejection. What are some baby steps you can take toward the hope of true relationship with your sisters in Christ?**

Chapter 2

"Women Are So Mean ..."

> *"Raise your hand if you have
> ever been personally victimized
> by Regina George."*
> Ms. Norbury, *Mean Girls*

It's been a month now in my new position as associate women's pastor; I haven't turned in my resignation letter, but there are four different drafts on my personal desktop because a person would be stupid to keep that on her work laptop. It's another Tuesday morning Bible study and I'm jiggling my keys into the stubborn door that never wants to open if it's colder than thirty-five degrees outside. My friend will be leading us in worship this morning, and she's rubbing her hands together to keep warm as we make our way inside and turn on the lights in advance of the rest of the band.

I'm in charge of all things technical so I get the sound booth ready and the instruments locked in. Right on cue, women start making their way to their seats as we finish up the final notes and finishing touches. My friend joins me in the sound booth as the room fills to capacity and I feel her shoulder touch mine. I'm still not emotionally prepared for anyone to say anything serious, so I turn to say something off topic and her eyes are wide, tears holding on to her eyelashes for dear life before one finally hits the top of her cheek.

She lowers her voice into a hushed whisper, barely moving her mouth in case there are any professional lip-readers in the room.

"Natalie, what if they do this to me? What if they send me here to do this with you? I can't be sent to women's ministry too," and she says this as if women's ministry is one level above the dark abyss of hell.

I don't know if I should be insulted; it's the first time someone has been honest about the bleakness of this transition. I am at a loss for words, so she does her best to recover quickly, linking her arm in mine. "I'm so sorry," she says. "I know you don't want this either. It's just women can be so mean! I don't know if I could do it ..."

I am oscillating between wanting to defend my new position to protect my pride and comforting my friend. Her reaction is raw and real. After all, women—in particular, church women—don't have the best reputation for friendliness, and we are surrounded by hundreds of them.

In our thirty-some years on the planet, we had not only read and believed the scripts that women were mean. We had seen it with our own eyes when we were younger.

Mean girls grew up to be mean women.

Gossip girls grew up to be women who would drag your name through the mud.

We're surrounded now by neutral puffy vests, Karen haircuts, and laughter that in our present mood we perceive as more cackling than good-natured. Holding on to each other tightly, we realize we are in the belly of the beast.

But we've been here before.

The Cafeteria Chronicles

I stand in the doorway of the middle school cafeteria, my senses overwhelmed by the echoing voices of three hundred eighth graders and the stench of the infamous Wednesday mystery meat dish wafting from the kitchen. My eyes scan the room looking for a place to land and I see a friend with a seat beside her, so I lower my eyes and quickly make a run for safety, hoping not to attract any unwanted attention.

"Oh, sorry, Natalie, I told Katie I would save this seat for her." My friend places her hand on the bench, looking over my shoulder at Katie, who is now edging past me to take the opening. My face grows warm as I survey other nearby seating options until Danielle, the queen bee of this particular hive, leans across the table and says, "Sorry, there's no room here. You can't sit with us. Go sit over there with Kelly and Amanda."

I look over my shoulder and see two girls I barely know sitting across from each other having an intense conversation at the end of a long, empty table placed against a cold wall. Without saying a word, I turn and slowly make my way toward them, wondering if

I will be a welcome addition or a third wheel. Much to my relief, they graciously invite me to join them, and for the rest of that year we spent every lunch playing card games, sharing food, and inviting others to be part of what felt like teenage rebellion: standing up to the cool kids.

Throughout my entire eighth-grade year, when I went to my locker, I was met with snide remarks reminding me where others thought I belonged and where I wasn't wanted. Every night, I fell asleep with tears flowing, begging my mom to homeschool me. But then at lunch I found myself laughing hysterically during a competitive game of Spoons, and one of the bees who had been exiled from her hive would make her way over to our table. And we made room because we understood: the pain of rejection comes from a deep desire for community and friendship.

Women want friendship and we also want to belong.

By the time I entered high school, I had learned that traditional educational systems were just one place that girls could be and would be mean and that nobody was safe from their gossip sessions or the rumor mill. A second place provided an equally inhospitable environment for many adolescent girls: the church youth group. What should have been a sanctuary from the everyday troubles of adolescent girlhood also presented unique challenges as we grew up together physically and spiritually under the watchful eyes of our mothers, each with their own past and relationship challenges with women.

Unfortunately for me, some of those same girls who wouldn't make room at tables in school were also active members of my church youth group, making it nearly impossible for me to escape.

I can remember one of the public-school queen bees showing up at summer youth group. I was mortified she would be sharing a cabin with me and my church friends at camp. I had told them how mean she had been to me, and they decided to take it upon themselves to make her miserable on my behalf. It was a week of whispering behind her back and making fun of what she wore, and for a while it felt good not to be the target.

But I also didn't like how it felt being the arrow.

Mean Girls and Gossip Girls

Mara Wilson writes in her book *Where Am I Now?*, "Mean girls come in all shapes and sizes. Some are blond cheerleaders, and some are Francophile brunettes who love Tim Burton and write song lyrics on their Converse. It was rarely the hellhounds who said anything mean to me; they expressed no real malice toward me other than the occasional eye roll. They were at the top and had nothing to gain by pushing me around."

She continues, "The ones who scared me, who still scare me, are the girls who see all other girls as competition, who see themselves as the persecuted ones, the ones whom the pretty and popular girls hate. When you believe you're persecuted, you will believe anything you do is justified."[1]

When I thought about this one mean girl at school who had followed me to youth camp, yes, she was quick to make me feel invisible and exclude me, but I knew she came from a difficult home life and that she watched how close my family was at church. I knew she struggled with insecurities different from mine and her biggest issue with me was that I was a "goody-goody" and always had to be "perfect." She never actually hurt me, yet here I was purposefully trying to make some sort of statement, and it didn't make me feel good. In fact, after two or three days of the constant teasing, I felt convicted that an eye for an eye wasn't Christlike or helpful in trying to establish a real friendship, which was the direction I preferred to take.

No, establishing true, sacred sisterhood would take time, patience, grace, trust, and taking risks, knowing that to love someone could mean opening up to potentially being hurt by them.

You and I, we will be one of the greatest risks we take in this lifetime.

But it can be exhausting… living a life of jockeying between popularity and anonymity, being invited and getting rejected, people knowing our name and others whispering it. It is easy to become paranoid anytime we walk into a room and a group of women look up and grow quiet. Wondering if they are talking about us. Choosing to believe the best but bracing ourselves for the worst.

Though past generations might have been caught off guard by the savage environment of high school, teens today seem less surprised that their public school system is filled with mean girls and gossip girls. Their TV shows and movies have humorously prepared them for the worst, and I've watched my own daughters and their peers go in ready for anything at the hands of those with whom they are desperate to belong. We live in a fallen world where people are inherently flawed and fight for positions and status into adulthood.

What I don't think any of us are prepared for, across the generational lines, is for this mean behavior to move from the movie screen into our junior high cafeteria, and on into the sanctuary. After all, the church should know better, and we should certainly do better.

> For many of us, stained-glass windows and padded pews just provide a prettier backdrop for the ugly behavior we endure.

Where school cafeterias allow queen bees to fly freely, shouldn't our church sanctuaries be a safe haven for those looking for sisterhood and friendship? Shouldn't we be able to show up with confidence and know we will be wanted, included, celebrated, and loved?

But for many of us, stained-glass windows and padded pews just provide a prettier backdrop for the ugly behavior we endure.

Building a Sanctuary of Sisterhood

Perhaps it has taken me half of a lifetime to understand we have the power to change not only our script, but to rebuild the set. I want my daughters and generations of young girls to experience sacred sisterhood in Christian community so when they walk into their public schools, colleges, and workplaces, they bring it with them. They will know what true friendship should look like and how to spot the imitations.

I want them to know they have the safety of the sanctuary when the rest of the world feels like it is betraying them.

So, what would a sanctuary of sisterhood look like for us as true disciples of Jesus Christ, as daughters of a Father who created us for friendship with one another?

Well, first of all, we need to be the most welcoming faces and encouraging voices in the House of God!

We will be steeples of strength and solidarity.

We will be pews filled with patience and perseverance to sit with those who are mourning, waiting, and wavering in their faith.

We will be open doors that welcome every sister no matter her appearance, her past, her present, her title, her vocation (or lack thereof), or her status in life.

We will be a baptism filled with Living Water.

We will be pulpits who speak Good News.

We will be altars who represent safety and rest.

We will be the hands and feet of Jesus, serving one another in every season without expecting anything in return.

From Gossip Girls to God's Girls

It took me a long time to understand that not everyone who called themselves a Christian was a true Christ follower. Jesus tells the disciples in John 13:35, "Your love for one another will prove to the world that you are my disciples."

First Corinthians 13:4–7 helps us understand what that love looks like by giving us an actual list:

> Love is patient and kind. Love is not jealous or boastful or proud or rude. It does not demand its own way. It is not irritable, and it keeps no record of being wronged. It does not rejoice about injustice but rejoices whenever the truth wins out. Love never gives up, never loses faith, is always hopeful, and endures through every circumstance.

I would come to understand that just because a girl sat in a pew or a woman taught a Sunday school class or called herself a pastor or youth leader didn't necessarily mean she was going to model biblical leadership, much less demonstrate sacred sisterhood.

My greatest hurts have come from gossip from those I thought loved me and Jesus. To this day, the walls I've worked so hard to break down through prayer and counseling go right back up the minute I find out my name has been on someone's lips with ill intent.

And when it's a friend or church member, it nearly crushes me every time.

Here's what I know: if someone is talking to you about someone, they are also talking to someone about you.

We all do it. But why?

If teenagers are gossiping, it's because their parents gossip. We teach our kids through thin walls and car rides more than we know.

The only way to kill the divisive weed is to starve it. To look the person in the eye and say, "Let's talk about something else," and pull it up by its root.

Our churches cannot be safe places when people know how to gossip more than pray. Even in our churches, mean women create mean girls.

Our small groups cannot be healthy or on mission if every prayer circle turns into a cackling crow's nest.

Jane Austen wrote, "Every man is surrounded by a neighborhood of voluntary spies."[2]

But it is my belief that sanctuaries—whether an actual church building or our home or local coffee shop—shouldn't tolerate voluntary spies, and if they are in the camp, they are exposed and brought to accountability.

Our tongues will either give life or take it, and we will be held accountable for every word thrown to sow discord.

I'll never forget sitting in my car in the parking lot at my youngest daughter's soccer practice on a warm spring night, the windows down. I watched my daughter have a conversation with another girl, and as she walked away, the coach asked the other little girl if they knew each other from school. Not knowing I was Selah's mom or that my window was wide open, I heard her mutter on her breath, "Sadly."

I was shocked! They were only in sixth grade. What on earth had my child done to make her respond that way?

Heart racing, I sat up taller in my driver's seat and took off my sunglasses so she could see into my seething soul. I leaned out the window, and as she ducked into her parents' car parked next to mine to grab water, I asked her, "Oh, you know my daughter from school?" Realizing I had heard everything, she looked up in complete horror, and her mom stared blankly over into my window.

"I heard you say 'sadly' so I just wanted to make sure Selah has been nice to you, since you gave such a strong reaction."

The mom was unfazed and rolled up her window, so from that moment on I knew I was dealing with a mean mom raising a mean girl. I asked Selah about it after practice. She shrugged it off saying they weren't really friends and she didn't care, but I could tell it was confusing for her. They didn't even know each other or share a class, but clearly something about my daughter made this other little girl react negatively. Selah and I talked it through and concluded we can't control how others treat us, but we can control how we treat others.

It's so easy for us as women to grow up holding on to the bitterness of feeling unseen, unwanted, and rejected from our childhood and then project those experiences onto our own children to protect them from the same fate.

If you're mean first, nobody can be mean to you.

If you're popular, nobody can hurt you.

Rewrite the Script

But what if healed, secure women created healed, secure girls?

What if we did the hard work of healing and forgiving and modeling what it looks like to be a woman who speaks life over others?

We could flip the script from gossip girl to God's girl. From a mean girl to a mentor, a girl who models speaking to one another after the way Jesus spoke to the disciples, after the way Jesus encouraged the disciples to speak to both friends and strangers.

In 1 Timothy 5:2 (MSG), Paul writes to Timothy and encourages him to "reverently honor an older woman as you would your mother, and the younger women as sisters."

Other scriptures instruct us to speak to one another not only as sisters in Christ but as the family of God.

"Watch the way you talk. Let nothing foul or dirty come out of your mouth. Say only what helps, each word a gift" (Eph. 4:29 MSG).

"Words kill, words give life; they're either poison or fruit—you choose" (Prov. 18:21 MSG).

"It's your heart, not the dictionary, that gives meaning to your words. A good person produces good deeds and words season after season. An evil person is a blight on the orchard. Let me tell you something: Every one of these careless words is going to come back to haunt you. There will be a time of Reckoning. Words are powerful; take them seriously. Words can be your salvation. Words can also be your damnation" (Matt. 12:34–37 MSG).

"Women Are So Mean ..."

I get that it's quite simple to google a few scriptures on the importance of speaking life and being women of integrity in how we choose to use our words. The balm of the gospel often stings when it first makes contact with an open wound.

When you're going through the loss of a good friend, a season of loneliness and mistrust, a lifetime of waiting for a friend who will love you unconditionally and stay by your side, the sentiment of verses like these is nice, but it doesn't feel obtainable.

It is painful when you've been the source of gossip and slander. I know what they said about you hurt. I know what poison feels like on fresh roots learning how to grow again, and how hard it is to nurse wilted petals that broke through rocky ground wanting desperately to believe new soil would produce new hope.

I know well that pit in my stomach and am too familiar with the hot tears of rejection and cold reception of my reputation.

But God. He comes now to each of us with redemption.

Because what was said about you is never as powerful as who he says you are and whose you are. His truth throws light on their shade. Don't grow weary in busting through dead places to bring life. Don't stop shining because someone said you shine too brightly. Let people talk and let God defend.

My hope is that as women we can change our conversations from bonding over the "I knows" of rejection and begin unifying over who we are and can become in Christ.

I KNOW I am wanted.

I KNOW I am accepted.

I KNOW I am loved.

I KNOW my soil.

And then we can unapologetically grow, individually and together.

Then we can be what we needed to other women who are on their own search for sacred sisterhood.

Flip Your Script

1. If you are honest, have you been the mean girl at times? Were you aware of how you were hurting others? Have you changed, or do you still feel a need to be the queen bee, the most popular at any cost, even as a grown woman?

2. Who were the mean girls of your past, and who are the mean girls of your present? How did these girls impact your view of women?

3. As we allow God to heal us from these wounds of our past, what are ways we can help other sisters heal? Maybe it's a word of encouragement to the mom who looks frazzled in the grocery store, a bouquet of flowers sent to a sister you know lost someone special, a visit to the widow next door who always yells at you for parking too close to her lawn. Words of life give life. Let's start there.

Chapter 3

"Women Are Such Drama Queens..."

"Stop creating drama, you're not Shakespeare."[3]

Melissa Harrison

Today is the day I move into my new office. They gave me a nice budget so I can have comfortable chairs and a couch for women to sit on when we meet for pastoral care—plus I get a brand-new desk. Everything is getting delivered around lunchtime and it's already ten o'clock, so I take my laptop, Bible, and journal to my empty office to wait for the delivery truck to arrive.

I open the pages in my journal. I bought a fresh leather-bound notebook at Target to document my journey in this position as associate women's pastor. I also bought new Flair pens, as if a new journal and new pens will rewrite this story into something easier to tell. I flip back a few entries and reread my words, a few spots blurry from where my tears hit the page before the ink had time to dry.

I spend an hour with myself, the fresh laments written to a melancholy minor-chord melody that matches the sorrow of Job and poetic stances of the book of Psalms. I'm ebbing and flowing with each emotion and reliving each conversation as if it will bring clarity to the confusion of this season, but as I flip to the next empty page, I can't help but shake my head as old scripts flood my mind, words spoken over me since I was a little girl ...

"Jeez, what a drama queen."

Am I the Drama?

I remember the moment I found out I was having my first baby girl and feeling simultaneous bliss and dread, as I was just nine years out of high school and the girl drama was still fresh in my brain. As I became a new mom, other mom friends in the throes of raising teen girls would feel it necessary to give me fair warning.

"Enjoy your girls now while they are chubby and tiny and can't talk back ..."

"Just wait until they are teenagers and sleep in until noon and only come down to eat and argue ..."

"I'm so glad I have sons; I've heard raising teenage girls is like living with drama 24/7 ..."

"Teen girls are *such* drama queens."

Didn't anyone have anything nice or encouraging to say about raising girls?

I was terrified I would raise drama queens, little performers who put on extreme emotional performances or reactions for attention, who overreact and overreach, and as a result draw every other drama queen in the land to our home.

I now have two teenage daughters, and my husband and I did our best to bring them into their elementary school years and junior high tween days with as little drama as possible. We employed strategies such as only allowing them to read books and watch shows that empowered them to be good friends and polite young ladies. We disciplined with grace and truth, we followed through with consequences to behavior that hurt a friend or stranger on the playground, and we taught them to respect adults and speak with kindness and intentionality.

They certainly aren't perfect. We've had our fair share of hard days following through with losing privileges and long evenings sitting at the ends of their beds, talking through why they wouldn't be attending a party or sleepover because of how they treated someone or spoke to me or their father.

Turns out, we have our fair share of dramatic flair in our home because teenagers in general bring with them an innocent hormonal drama that can be invitational and engaging when channeled properly.

When my oldest was just starting to hang out in mixed groups of both male and female classmates, she was excited to finally be having that teen-movie high school experience. Before I knew it, kids were coming through our door at all hours, and both my husband and I were enjoying the variety of personalities.

However, there was always one girl in the mix who was all about the drama. Her reactions to everything were *huge*, her voice loud and echoing over all the others. No one could get a word in even if you tried, and before long, people (including myself) just stopped trying. She was larger than life and my daughter began to show me the text threads that were dominated with boy drama, family drama, sports drama, school drama, and life drama ... all *drama*.

My daughter grew exhausted trying to manage the late-night texts and FaceTime calls, suddenly evolving into a peer counselor more than a friend, and I was exhausted for her. It was too much for her sixteen-year-old heart to handle and suddenly everything went from innocent and fun to serious and laced with complicated storylines and exaggerated emotion.

Raising our teenage girls effortlessly took me back to my own teen years and revealed my flaws, because after all, hindsight truly is 20/20. I couldn't deny that I myself had been drawn to drama, chasing after the juiciest gossip and newest breakups because it made me feel part of something.

Something inside of me had needed the drama and attention.

When that young lady had been in our home, I saw part of myself in her and my heart ached for whatever wasn't fulfilled inside of her.

Many times, drama queens are internally lost little girls looking for someone to validate the sound of their voice after years of feeling silenced or ignored over important issues that directly impact their lives and the lives of those they love. They haven't had anyone model self-awareness or self-control for them, and if they have had that modeled, no one has held them accountable or course corrected them when they demand an audience—the laughter, the response, the reaction.

When we say, "Girls are such drama queens," we are painting a broad stroke across an entire gender that doesn't leave room for nuance or emotion.

Yes, constantly being in the presence of someone with high emotions without the maturity to wisely manage them can be exhausting, but the answer isn't to silence or shame the person because friendship with them will require shouting to be heard.

Rather, subduing drama requires a breaking of bad habits and silencing lies spoken over girls, not crushing their spirit because of our inability to tolerate their flair for frenzy. We want women to feel as though they are a reliable narrator in the story God has been writing for them, not as if their voices are annoying—like nails down a chalkboard.

We should find what makes them come alive and then give them a megaphone through friendship. We can contend with them for what breaks their hearts so they know they aren't alone.

It's offering them a cool cup of water rather than blasting them with a fire extinguisher.

And I know this because *I am a fellow drama queen.*

Not because I had absentee parents or a mom who didn't adore me. I was surrounded by good people who believed in me and told me I could be anything I wanted to be! And I believed them.

In my youth, my dramatic flair wasn't out of brokenness but more from a lack of humility. I thought everything I had to say was important. I liked having a platform. I enjoyed debate team and speech competitions with their captive audiences, but I lacked the emotional intelligence to understand the right time and place.

Emotional intelligence is the ability to perceive, use, understand, manage, and handle emotions. When you have high EI, you can manage and recognize your own emotions and those of others around you, taking in all the social cues around you to guide your thinking and behavior, discerning feelings, assigning them appropriately, and adjusting your emotions to adapt to ever-changing environments.

Early on in my ministry and corporate settings alike, I did not exhibit great emotional intelligence. Nobody ever corrected me, and I would unknowingly steamroll through a room without even realizing I had silenced introverts, unfairly commanded attention without earning trust, and demanded respect without offering it first as a new voice in the room.

Eventually in the course of my career, I encountered a difficult church staff situation. I came into an environment where I wasn't being well received by the female staff, and part of it was my fault. I truly wanted to fit in and be part of a family that didn't necessarily want me or trust me yet. Thankfully, my leadership assigned me a one-on-one, six-week mentorship session with an emotional intelligence guru.

This coaching Yoda drew awareness for me that, although unfair, my physical characteristics might cause a room to draw conclusions about me from the way I dress, my height, hair color, posture, eye contact, and body language. I was shocked. Being a 5'9" brunette of muscular build came with preconceived notions I had been completely unaware of. I had worked so hard to overcome my own insecurities and be confident in my height and weight, build, broad shoulders, but now I was hearing that these things made me appear "intimidating," "power hungry," and "demanding," all of which were the total opposite of my personality.

At first, I felt defeated and offended.

I quickly learned that simply being a woman would put labels on me I couldn't escape. Many of these imposed labels would create barriers in leading teams, making friends, and doing something as crucial as my job. It felt like even greater rejection coming from the church community where we were to be patient and long-suffering with one another's shortcomings.

What I learned at forty years old was revolutionary for me as a woman who leads others. Emotional intelligence wasn't just managing my own emotions in changing environments and relationships, but also increasing my awareness of the emotions of others as I used social cues to regulate my speech patterns, tone, volume, and means of suggesting change in spaces where I hadn't yet acquired trust.

While my friends and those who had known me a long time knew I was a bottom-line person who liked to get things done and resorted to humor and sarcasm to put people at ease, I learned I needed to manage, not kill, my inner drama queen and seek to understand before demanding to be understood.

> Women, we are all a little drama and a little queen at times.

Women, we are all a little drama and a little queen at times.

True sisters in Christ are willing to sit in the tension of the tears and tiaras with one another as we grow and mature in our relationship with God and one another.

When the Mamas Are the Drama

Because of prior experiences in both the workplace and church, I had to overcome my own prejudices against women. Many of my beliefs about my own gender developed at a very young age from the women in my family as well as the women who surrounded my friends. Each of their moms came with their own unique style of mothering and often projected their dysfunction onto me when I was under their care.

One summer my Girl Scout troop was given the opportunity to attend an overnight horse camp, the first time I had been away from my family for more than a night or two. I can remember being nervous, insecure even among friends, trying so hard to be brave and connect with the other moms on the trip who dressed a little fancier, always looking like they stepped out of a JCPenney catalogue or a family portrait.

They had known me since I was in kindergarten, but that's what is so interesting about women (as I learned through coaching): we often mistake proximity for intimacy. The danger in this is assuming we have relationship to speak hard things, to make corrections, or to demand vulnerability from those with whom we have not fully earned their trust. It's through these lessons unpacked in counseling, coaching, and even with other women further along in life that we are able to be more careful in how we speak and engage with one another in everyday interactions.

As I sat at the rally's outdoor restaurant with my sandwich and French fries surrounded by my troop, I was unusually quiet, which drew the attention of one of the moms I always thought looked just like a Midwest Martha Stewart: beautiful blond hair, porcelain skin, thin frame, collared shirts French tucked into her fitted khaki shorts belted with a brand-name leather accessory.

"Natalie, you're quiet today. Are you okay?"

Her concern felt genuine, and for a moment I felt my guard let down, but rather than confess I was feeling homesick and a little sad, I just told her I had a headache.

I'll never forget her response. On that hot summer day in front of all the other moms and girls at the table, she shook her head and said with a smirk, "Oh, Natalie, you have always been such a hypochondriac."

I felt my face flush and my heart sink. Is that what they thought about me? Every unknown fear and insecurity I had about what these moms might say behind my back or to their daughters became the new script. I pushed my tray away and laid my head—now pulsing and hot—down on my arms as I fought off tears. Nobody wanted a hypochondriac *and* a crybaby on this trip.

For whatever reason, this specific conversation is branded into my memory as if it were yesterday. Of all the good and positive words that have been spoken over me by other moms and would be spoken over me in the years to come, this one still burns. It marked me, and now as a mom myself, I am careful of the things I speak over my daughters' friends every time they come through our door.

We are so glad you're here. Our home is your home. We are so thankful for your friendship with our daughter. You are a blessing to our family. You are so creative. You are beautiful inside and out. You feel like you just belong here.

I am aware of how I show up to sporting events, school outings, field trips, birthday parties, and in church. I always assume there are eyes on me, the eyes of a daughter looking for words of life and hope to be spoken over her. And, if offered, a hug, a nod of approval, a "good job," or "I see you" with a smile and pat on the back. Because even if every other woman in her life is good and supportive and loving, our reinforcement models a deep-seated desire that other women can be and should be our greatest place of safety and friendship in the world, but more importantly in the church.

Women, let me remind you that you are directly and indirectly affecting every female who comes into your presence. It isn't just in the way you talk to them, but how you parent, how you treat others, and how you show up and carry yourself in public. Little eyes are watching you in the grocery store, at the public pool, listening to how you speak about and to your own daughters and taking note of how you handle conflict, troubleshoot, handle adversity, and receive compliments. If you ever wanted an audience, you have one, but less on a stage and more like hidden cameras behind the eyes of women young and old desperately hoping you will be different from some of the other women they have encountered. If it feels like a huge responsibility, that's because it is. It only takes one careless remark to brand another woman for the rest of her life.

> **It only takes one careless remark to brand another woman for the rest of her life.**

Rewrite the Script

While some moms will be the drama, others will unapologetically put an end to the drama the moment their child is involved.

As I was a pastor's kid, the church moms of my teenage female peers were often jealous of what they perceived to be favor or special treatment I received. Their reaction cut me deeply and created this theme in my life that church women couldn't be trusted.

I left so many church events early because of the backhanded comments made about my sister or me, and I watched my own mom keep her anger at bay. Until one night, my mom had enough of the drama and put an end to the show from the back porch of the church parsonage.

I had been attending a youth campout behind the church, and as we settled in and it got colder, I decided to go back to our house next to the church for the rest of the night. I remember telling our youth pastor, who was the mom of another student, that I wanted to sleep in my own bed. She exploded into a rage with all the reasons why I would feel entitled to do so.

Women, when other young women respectfully draw boundaries and make their own decisions that are in their best interest, it isn't in competition with your authority. It is a young person doing their best to practice making adult decisions that are safe and reasonable—and most likely with purpose. Her response made me flee from the campsite in tears, unsure of what provoked her reaction, straight to my house and into the arms of my mom.

Sometimes, we can save ourselves from unnecessary drama by giving each other the benefit of the doubt, even when our pride or preferences are challenged.

Having enough of the accumulating events that had led to this final moment, my mom ran to the back porch of the church parsonage and screamed as loud as she could into the night air for anyone who might hear her mama cry, "You are just a bunch of HYPOCRITES!"

Though I am quite confident not a soul could hear her tearful rebuke, it meant so much to me as her daughter. It wasn't particularly effective, and it wouldn't change our situation, but I felt defended and fought for. To this day, every now and then, my sister or I will remind our mom of that fall night in the countryside by randomly texting "hypocrites!" without any context.

> We can be the showstoppers, closing the curtain before the performance even begins. We don't create the drama; we shut it down.

Now that I'm a mom, I get it. We can be the showstoppers, closing the curtain before the performance even begins. We don't create the drama; we shut it down. And we remind ourselves that we are to be women who defend and fight for peace in chaos.

I pray you know you have a showstopper in me. I pray I have a showstopper in you.

May we all stand on the back porches of our spiritual homes and through passionate rebuke dismantle every word curse and every lie that has been spoken over our sisters.

May the enemy rue the day he set us against one another.

Flip Your Script

1. Are you the drama? Have you at one time or another used theatrics to get attention?

2. When thinking about emotional intelligence, are you aware of the impact you make on others when you walk into a room or engage in conversation? Are you someone who steamrolls over others to be heard, or are you more likely to get quiet when others get loud?

3. What is your response to the drama queens in your home, work, and church? You can either buy a ticket to the show or pull the curtain; how you engage impacts you and those around you.

Chapter 4

"Women Are So Insecure..."

"For the LORD is your security."
Proverbs 3:26

"Hey, Pastor Natalie, does all this furniture belong to you?"

I look up from my journal to see a few of our hospitality guys rolling a cart with large boxes from the hall into my doorway. My eyes light up with excitement. Wait, is this happiness I am feeling?

They help me unload my treasures, and it isn't until they are well on their way back down the hall that I realize something isn't adding up. I had ordered two chairs, a couch, and a desk, but sitting here in my office isn't furniture—rather, several boxes filled with *pieces* of furniture.

I grab a pair of scissors and cut away at the tape of each one to pile little plastic baggies of screws and Allen wrenches, wood panels with dots labeled with letters, and tiny wooden pegs at my feet. My happiness immediately turns back to anxiety and frustration as I slump down against the wall, draw my knees to my chest, and muster up every ounce of energy for the long day ahead of me.

"Knock, knock." I look up to see another pastor, Jacqui, at my door with her sleeves rolled up, holding the hammer she keeps in her drawer to hang pictures of her new grandbaby on her walls. She's sturdy, a military wife who has moved more times than she can count, experienced at taking things apart only to have to put them back together again.

I don't want to accept her help. After all, shouldn't I know how to put together a few pieces of furniture? I feel so needy, like a college kid moving into my freshman dorm, but she's already got part of the desk put together and I am desperate for assistance and some company, so I grab the Allen wrench and clumsily pretend as if I know what I am doing.

This wasn't the first time I felt insecure in front of a peer ...

The Great Pumpkin

It was October 1997; my sister and I weren't allowed to trick-or-treat and usually spent our Halloween nights either hiding in our dark house pretending we weren't home or at the annual church Hallelujah party dressed as an angel or a Bible parable.

Maybe it was because I was a senior, or because my mom was growing soft as we aged, but when my school friends suggested we all come dressed up for our final Halloween as high schoolers, my mom agreed to let me participate. I showed up Halloween morning dressed like a giant orange pumpkin, complete with tights, a hat, and my face painted bright orange for extra dramatic flair.

I made sure to be super early so we could snag a few photos with our disposable cameras for our senior photo albums, and the minute I walked into the commons area, I knew something was very wrong. Everything felt as if it were moving in slow motion, like I could actually feel the world spinning in real time around me, and I stood in the middle of the room not sure if I should laugh or cry.

My girlfriends, who had suggested we dress up, came running to me, wearing normal, everyday clothing as if we hadn't made a pact just a few days ago. (In the days before cell phones, there were no group texts or social media DMs to let one know of last-minute changes of plans.)

"Oh my gosh, Natalie! You look amazing. We totally forgot ..."

"I am so sorry we didn't remember ..."

I wasn't sure if I should believe them or not; I just knew I had to get out of that commons area without creating any more of a scene, so I ran my giant orange butt down the hallway toward the bathroom where I hid until the homeroom bell rang.

I weighed all my options. My parents worked full-time and couldn't bring me normal clothes. Even if they did, half the school had already seen me. It would take hours to get my face back to its normal color. But I couldn't just go home. I had midterm exams as well as a Hamlet monologue due in my theater class, which I would be forced to execute as a giant gourd.

My entire high school career I had worked hard to not draw attention to myself, to fit in and be like all the other girls. I had hated my body, my hair, and my wardrobe for so long and thought if I could look like everyone else and follow the high school script, I could be that popular girl like in all the movies. But deep down, I wasn't like everyone else, and I knew it.

I remember looking in the mirror at my tear-streaked face and making a decision that would, believe it or not, change my life. I grabbed the orange face paint out of my backpack and touched up my cheeks, straightened my crooked stem hat, and marched myself out into the crowded hallway where I was met with some funny stares but also a chorus of, "Cool costume!" "Wow, you're so brave!" and "I would have dressed up too—you should have told me!"

Suddenly, I wasn't invisible, but it was okay.

And my fifth-period Shakespeare class got the performance of a lifetime.

Sequined Soliloquies

That day changed the way I spoke to myself, about myself, and how I saw myself. I would still struggle with insecurity from time to time, but in this pivotal moment I decided if I could survive an entire day dressed as a giant pumpkin, I could do anything—well, within reason. Throughout high school, my well-intended teachers had pulled me aside and encouraged me to be more confident as I hid in my oversized sweatpants and T-shirts. I had struggled for years with body dysmorphia, my journals filled with poems of how it felt to live in a body I knew was healthy but not skinny.

The '90s weren't exactly kind to young women, with heroin chic fashion gracing the covers of our most popular magazines. Many of us found ways to avoid food and hide our addictions. To this day, I know many women who were teen girls at that time who continue to have a very complicated relationship with food and exercise.

I remember going home that day, taking off the giant pumpkin costume, and reflecting on how shocked my classmates and perfect strangers reacted to it all.

They thought I was *brave? Funny? Unique? Creative?*

Wait, I *was* all those things!

I had to change my inner monologue—the way I spoke to myself when I looked into the mirror or before a big presentation, or while waiting for a guy to pick me up. It mattered. In my attempt to have model behavior and fit into a mold everyone could accept, I had dulled my sparkle. It wasn't anyone's fault but my own.

Women, the way we speak to ourselves and about ourselves matters and directly affects how we speak to each other and about each other.

Now a mom in my forties, the way my body looks and feels has drastically changed, and I have accepted the reality that I can still be healthy and fit, but my twenty-year-old figure is long gone. In a conversation with a friend whom I hadn't seen in a year, she complimented the hard work I was putting in at the gym. But rather than receive her comment with gratitude, I met it with a disclaimer.

"Girl, I've still got so much work to do. Look at this belly!"

She raised her pointer finger at me and said, "Hey, be nice how you talk about my friend Natalie; she's beautiful."

And I was immediately convicted.

My inner monologue was exposed in a dialogue with a friend who saw me as a sister and daughter of God—perfectly created—and she wasn't going to let me talk about myself like that in her presence.

Her correction that morning stuck with me, and I was reminded that just as eighteen-year-old Natalie found freedom dressed as a pumpkin on a cold Halloween morning in 1997, this was a season of embracing every line and curve I had earned since.

My prayer for us all is that we would be aware of the way we speak to ourselves and fully love who we have become, in the face of adversity and life in general. Out of the abundance of the heart, the mouth speaks, and just as my mom used to tell me, "It doesn't matter if you're pretty on the outside if you're ugly on the inside."

Take a good look in the mirror, sweet sister.

Be careful how you talk about her and to her.

That's my friend, and she's beautiful.

Identity Crisis

Though our identities as females might start in our youth with our fashion choices or mishaps, true identity lies far beyond what can be seen. The Scriptures tell us that while people will look at our outward appearance, God is looking at our heart, and from the abundance of the heart the mouth speaks. When we are insecure, when we fail to understand who we are and to whom we belong, the condition of our hearts eventually will leak out of our speech and actions as we are warned in Matthew chapter 12 verse 34: "For whatever is in your heart determines what you say."

> God is looking at our heart, and from the abundance of the heart the mouth speaks.

When our identity and security is wrapped up in what we do, we become insecure and fearful that if we lose a title or position, we will lose influence among those we lead because we have placed power in perception.

After spending twenty years leading worship and finding my identity and security (my worth) in what I did for God, not who I was in Christ, the move from worship ministry to women's ministry hit me personally. For the longest time I didn't tell those closest to me that I was no longer on the worship staff; I didn't post anything about my new role or share the transition because I associated being a worship pastor with my identity.

What would people think or say?

In my new office, in my new role, I felt exposed, like high school Natalie showing up in a pumpkin costume giving a Shakespeare monologue without any context.

"Wait, why isn't she leading worship anymore?"

"Is this what you wanted?"

"How did this happen?"

Every question felt like an interrogation, and my insecurities were louder than ever before as I tried to hold on to what had clearly become an idol.

The enemy can quickly turn something that started off with good and godly intentions into something we worship and love more than God himself. My identity as a worship pastor had become more important to me than my identity in Christ. That was why I was struggling to not only accept this new position but to love the women he had entrusted to me.

I couldn't see it for the gift that it was, and had it not been for mentors in my life who dragged me kicking and screaming into this new season—and a good Father who had his best in mind for me—I might have missed this opportunity to step into a beautiful new space with his daughters and my fellow sisters.

What are you holding on to right now as your security blanket that God might be asking you to surrender to him?

Maybe you've been known as the mom who can do it all. You have raised your kiddos and been room mom every year in their classrooms, baking their birthday cakes from scratch and hosting all the after-parties and events, cheering them on through every sporting event, and as the nest starts to empty you aren't quite sure who you are anymore. Your identity and security were found in being a mom and you're still a mom but with older children, your role and influence gradually changing in their lives. *What is God asking you to grab hold of now that is new and scary but part of this new season?*

Maybe you've always worked a traditional 9–5 job, and your identity has been wrapped up in promotions and status, your security in your salary, and now that you are closing in on retirement you can't fathom losing your title as CEO, office manager, team lead, principal, doctor, lawyer, the one everyone trusts to put out fires and handle bottom lines. *What if God is asking you to partner financially and/or spiritually with this next generation, to invest and intercede as a confidante and trusted advisor?*

Perhaps your identity has been wrapped up in being an artist, musician, caretaker, entrepreneur, innovator, risk-taker, influencer, and you can feel all the hopes and dreams of your youth slipping between your fingers. Bills have to be paid, life isn't a reality TV show, nobody is coming with a big check or a big break, and you realize you have to grow up and get a normal job. *What if what you perceive to be a punishment from God is an invitation to a season of order where he will align you with others to help you build something beautiful through wisdom and fiscal responsibility? What if doing the mundane is the beginning of the extraordinary?*

Sister, you are more than what you do for God. Your worth lies in being a co-heir with Christ who has a seat at the table of the Almighty King, who owns the cattle on a thousand hills, and you lack nothing. Your security is found in your eternal home, not your earthly assignment. Your value is in what you store in heaven, not here on this earth.

By knowing who we are in Christ, it is possible to go through life without suffering an identity crisis or deep insecurity.

Fully loved.

Fully equipped.

Fully trusted.

Rewrite the Script

I pull out a glittering necklace from the gallon-sized Ziploc bag of costume jewelry I'd brought with me all the way from Cincinnati to Mazatlán, Mexico, and the eyes of the young woman I have spent the day with getting her ready for her friend's quinceañera party grow wide with excitement.

We've spent a week with these precious young women recently rescued from a sex trafficking ring, their home a cinder block–type dormitory with everything they would need to grow and be kept safe. Swimming, hiking, making crafts, singing worship music, hearing their stories—we had packed the week full of all their favorite things, and this morning we had started early with our curling irons, hair straighteners, and makeup palettes in tow as we prepared for our final night tonight.

I lower the necklace over her head and gently clasp it at the nape of her neck. She barely flinches at my touch after a week of conversation and living some life together. I wonder if it gets any easier, trusting there are people who are for you and mean you no harm. I walk around her side and sit across from her, picking up the straightener and gliding it through a few more strands of her coarse black hair for final touches as the heat forms beads of sweat on both our brows.

She looks up at me as I step back to take it all in, not just her beauty but the miracle of her life, a girl physically and spiritually snatched from the jaws of death now safe and secure. I tear up and she smiles ear to ear as I have her stand and spin, her dress twirling, the sequins creating dancing rainbow prisms on the wall.

"Eres hermosa," I say, meaning, "You're beautiful."

She looks down at first and then raises her eyes to mine.

"Eres hermosa, pro dentro y por fuera."

"You're beautiful, both inside and out."

It wouldn't be the last time I would spend time with women who had gone from having a family and a name to being taken, sold, and branded with a number, from daughter to slave overnight. To see the burns seared into their backs and arms was a cruel reminder of a day they lost their identity and home. Yet with the day of their freedom in the warmth of the safe house with other women reminding them who they were, but more importantly *whose* they were, life was coming back into their eyes and hope danced cautiously back into their hearts.

But rewriting these scripts would take time, patience, prayer, and an entourage of women dedicated to their healing and care.

You and I may not carry physical reminders of the moments we lost our identity or security in who we are or whose we are, but it overflows in how to treat other women and even how to speak about ourselves.

We can read all the self-help books, go to all the conferences, watch all the videos, and hit every milestone we're supposed to hit as successful, influential women according to this world, but without Jesus it is meaningless. It is good to have goals and to find opportunities to be our healthiest, most confident selves, but it should never be at the expense of becoming selfless.

Sharon Hodde Miller writes, "For many of us, the source of our insecurity is *self-preoccupation*. What we need isn't to think more highly of ourselves, but to think of ourselves less."[4]

Personally, I've never felt more lost than when trying to find myself in a world that was never meant to be my home.

What we thought would bring us security only made us more insecure.

What we failed to realize is that it's good to take care of ourselves but for the hope of helping to take care of others.

When we blindly follow the script and believe the lies of this world, we will find ourselves in narratives never intended for us. God has written us a beautiful story. Though not perfect, his story offers protection and provision found in his Word that reminds us that the mirror is just a piece of glass.

By cutting out parts of the script that don't match the heart of our Father, we can see the sacred storyline much clearer.

> By cutting out parts of the script that don't match the heart of our Father, we can see the sacred storyline much clearer.

When heaven is the goal, the people we have been entrusted to lead and love become the prize.

God loves us. God loves you.

God's love isn't found in our success, relationship status, the latest diet, the newest fad. His love never fails, never changes, and when we really know how much we are loved, it changes the way we see ourselves and the way we see others.

Rewriting the script, debunking the lies that we have believed that our identity and security are wrapped up in looks, our friends, our jobs or financial status will require believing we are deeply loved and accepted by God, the One who created us, and God makes no mistakes. He loves our every imperfection, seen and unseen, and calls us his daughters.

God's love ...

- never gives up.
- cares more for others than for self.
- doesn't want what it doesn't have.
- doesn't strut.
- doesn't have a swelled head.
- doesn't force itself on others.
- isn't always "me first."
- doesn't fly off the handle.
- doesn't keep a score of the sins of others.
- doesn't revel when others grovel.
- takes pleasure in the flowering of truth.
- puts up with anything.
- trusts God always.
- always looks for the best.
- never looks back.
- keeps going to the end. (1 Cor. 13:4–8 MSG)

For some of us, understanding God's love and growing in our identity as his daughters might require us getting out of the comfort of our own home, ring light, social media account, city, country, and sitting across from someone who has truly had their identity stolen. Hearing their stories behind the scars, sitting in the discomfort of something so sacred we are forced to silence our inner critic and allow the Holy Spirit to use us to love someone the way Christ loves us.

But the only way we can truly love one another is to know how much Christ loves us.

This kind of love is for each of us, and we are called to extend this same love toward one another: for he is our help and our defender.

In him, we are secure.

Flip Your Script

1. In what ways were you insecure as a little girl? As a teenager? What about now?

2. How have you allowed those insecurities to keep you from friendship?

3. What are some lies that have been spoken over you by others who meant to hurt you or put you in your place? What are truths God has spoken over you that cancel out those lies? Write them down, put them somewhere you can see them every day. His Word is the better word.

Chapter 5

"Women Are So Jealous ..."

> *"Isn't it kind of silly to think that tearing someone else down builds you up?"*[5]
>
> Sean Covey, *The 7 Habits of Highly Effective Teens*

"Well, it seems as if they would rather have you doing all the promotional media for women's events moving forward."

I can detect the iciness in my boss's voice as she communicates the news from our creative team.

I'm honored and also confused; I don't want more visibility, and I certainly haven't asked for it. I've been in this position for nearly a year now, and I don't know if it's the new journal, the new pens, my new sturdy furniture, or Jesus, but I actually like a few of the women God has brought into my life since beginning this position.

I've been spending a lot of time in spiritual direction and mentorship as well as receiving wise, biblical counsel from close friends and family, and even though it's a daily surrender to choose to believe my identity is in Christ and not in what I do, I can feel a change happening in my heart that I suppose others can see too.

I've been given some speaking opportunities in other ministries in the church, which is a new tool God is teaching me to use.

Sort of like Jacqui with her hammer knew how to use what was in her hand to help me, I was learning to use what was in mine. Only now it felt like what I carried might cause unintentional tension between me and my boss.

I'm standing in her office door, not sure if I should say thank you for the opportunity, or I am sorry to have taken her opportunity away. All I know is I don't like the way it feels, and I'm suddenly very aware my mentor sees me as her competition.

The Price of Envy

"Mirror, mirror, here I stand. Who is the fairest in the land?"

Since we were little girls, envy has been an underlying cause for most of the conflict found in the storylines of our favorite Disney cartoons. From the wicked queen in *Snow White* asking her mirror to rank her beauty against others in the kingdom to the wicked stepmother in *Cinderella* who was so threatened by her stepdaughter's beauty that she made her work night and day until she was covered in soot and ashes, determined she would not go to the ball where she might meet her Prince Charming.

At a young age we all wanted to be the princess, but what we didn't realize was we were one bad day away from becoming the wicked queen.

Jealousy discriminates against no one.

It is the wart at the end of our nose, and there is no concealer on the market that can cover it up.

But Disney wasn't the first to give us fair warning of the price of envy. In the complicated relationship between Cain and Abel, the offspring of Adam and Eve, we see this struggle infiltrate the bond of brotherhood. As early as Genesis chapter 4, it is evident those we are meant to live among, those with whom we share a family tree, have the potential for both our greatest fellowship and our greatest betrayal.

The story of these blood brothers in Scripture gives us enough information to know that Cain was a farmer and Abel a herdsman. When it came time to present their sacrifices to the Lord, Cain brought the fruit of the ground and Abel the firstborn of his flock (Gen. 4:3–4). God accepted and favored Abel's offering but did not accept Cain's offering.

Hebrews 11:4 says, "By an act of faith, Abel brought a better sacrifice to God than Cain" (MSG).

Though scholars have made speculations as to why God preferred Abel's offering over Cain's, one thing is certain: God's rejection of Cain's sacrifice and acceptance of Abel's offering caused great jealousy in Cain's heart, which compelled him to murder his brother, Abel.

Though this isn't a female relationship, breaking our relationship with God in the garden brought many consequences including jealousy, comparison, envy, and other factors that divided and divorced the family of God.

The Bible is very clear about the repercussions of an envious heart. "You shall not covet your neighbor's house. You shall not covet your neighbor's wife, or his male or female servant, his ox or donkey, or *anything that belongs to your neighbor*" (Ex. 20:17 NIV).

In James we are given clear warning: "You want what you don't have, so you scheme and kill to get it. You are jealous of what others have, but you can't get it, so you fight and wage war to take it away from them. Yet you don't have what you want because you don't ask God for it. And even when you ask, you don't get it because your motives are all wrong—you want only what will give you pleasure" (4:2–3).

Jealousy will kill us one way or the other and bring death to those it touches.

When we look at someone and covet what they have, watch for them to fall, or delight in their failure, it only brings death to our own heart and soul.

Jealousy will always pervert that which is pure.

You and I look into a phone mirror every morning assessing who seems to be the fairest of them all. Who has the most success, money, fame, favor, visibility, followers? And we're like Joseph's brothers annoyingly staring at another's robe wondering if our Father loves us that much too.

We're Saul watching David returning from battle while the masses celebrate the tens of thousands David has defeated, and we're quick to draw swords and assign motive.

Jealousy throws our sisters into pits and makes us hunt those we have been assigned to run beside.

Let all of these examples be a cautionary tale that if we aren't careful, we will waste precious time thwarting the assignments of others and end up abandoning our own. We're looking into the mirrors of the world asking for validation rather than looking into the eyes of our image maker who has good things for all his daughters. One sister's perceived success takes nothing away from us. God's favor doesn't run out; he has plenty for us all.

A jealous sister cannot be a generous sister.

May God grant us the grace to walk out our assignments with heads down and eyes on him—not to our left or right. May we be palace dwellers in a world of pit pushing.

From Pauper to Princess

When I say, "Women are so jealous," I know it's true because I'm speaking from my own experience. I deal with my own jealous heart at times. For me to overcome this sin in my own life, in how I look at other women and speak of them, I must take a good look at myself through the eyes of my Father, and oftentimes it's my own inner reflection that is wicked.

As I mentioned before, my mom used to tell my sister and me that it didn't matter if we were pretty on the outside if we were ugly on the inside. You can be the most aesthetically pleasing person to look at, but eventually you will be unable to hide the warts growing from the inside out.

To this day I struggle with jealousy in different areas of my life. I am often jealous of my friends of a similar age who don't struggle with their weight. As a mom, I am jealous of women who seemingly have it all together, managing their time and families with ease. As a wife, I get jealous of the fancy date nights and extravagant vacations others post on Instagram. As a woman who writes and preaches, I am often jealous of my counterparts who always hit bestseller lists and speak at the biggest conferences.

I can feel myself being pulled off mission by the jealousy that comes from comparing myself, which leads to making me feel something that isn't who I am as a daughter of God. Yet I'm validated by the evil roots of jealousy if I sit in it long enough.

Well, they have famous parents.

Well, they have hundreds of thousands of followers.

Well, she doesn't have to work.

Well, she has a nanny.

Well, they've always been rich.

These justifying thoughts become comparison traps that not only diminish the success and joy of a sister but deny the very gifts from my generous Father who has met every single one of my needs and given me the desires of my heart.

"Anger is cruel, and wrath is like a flood, but jealousy is even more dangerous" (Prov. 27:4).

The antidote to our jealousy is developing empathy and compassion toward our sisters, especially those who have had to endure incredibly difficult situations. We may think they are thriving based on the highlight reels of social media, but they are likely just getting by like the rest of us.

When I first started writing books and traveling to speak and preach, I would often see other women posting about their success doing the same and feel a twinge when they sold more books, hit more bestseller lists, or received more likes on their reels. I hated my reaction.

> **The antidote to our jealousy is developing empathy and compassion toward our sisters.**

Then, one morning as I was mindlessly scrolling, I found myself watching another female communicator who was getting a lot of attention, and I felt that ugly, familiar spirit begin to creep in. As I learned more about her, what I discovered broke my heart. Her husband had recently passed, and she was now walking out the unimaginable—a fear many of us as wives and moms hold in the deep places of our hearts—yet she was still somehow showing up and preaching with such grace and anointing.

She had lost this most precious person, and I imagine she would trade all the platforms and success in the world to get him back, yet through the mourning and grief God was using her to bring comfort and joy to so many.

I was immediately convicted. Jealousy robs us of the opportunity to sit in sacred spaces with one another, to celebrate and mourn uninvited and unplanned seasons. I had no idea what her daily life must entail; I only saw the highlight reels from a church social media manager, not nearly enough information to justify entertaining the slightest bit of envy.

Cinderella, Snow White, Sleeping Beauty, Ariel, Jasmine. None of them had it all together when we first hear their stories. They were locked up in castles and told who they were and what they would become by others who did not fully understand their dreams or potential. If they had started out with everything, there wouldn't be a story for us to follow. Too often we start in the middle of the story, seeing what we believe is a happily ever after, but we haven't taken the time to explore or try to understand the opening chapters.

We would never be jealous of a sister's loss, pain, persecution, or tragedy. We envision walking in her glass slippers—not her house shoes—yet the journey from orphan to princess, maid to maiden, widow to mother in the House of God is the beautiful place where God meets us.

I want to be the kind of sister who walks with another from the tower to the castle and celebrates each step we take together toward her calling. But in order for me to do that, I have to stop wishing for what they have and focus on what I've been given so my own story can be written.

She's Just Jealous ...

I cannot tell you how many times this was said to me as a teenage girl whenever another girl was mean to me or just indifferent. "She's just jealous because everyone likes you ..." "She's just jealous because of how smart you are ..." "She's just jealous ..." Fill in the blank; you get what I'm saying.

As a strong athlete, good student, and overall nice person, my older daughter has already had her fair share of challenging relationships with girls. In an effort to bring her comfort, I've caught myself almost saying this very thing to her. But I stop myself before it leaves my mouth because while we want to be liked, approachable, easy to connect with, and invited into friendship, at the end of the day, we don't want to think people are jealous of us.

If someone is jealous of you, it makes it difficult to become friends and maintain a healthy relationship. So, to be someone other women are jealous of because of opportunities we've been given or personality traits we cannot turn off could mean a life of loneliness and isolation.

I don't want my daughter to stop being a loyal teammate, a good player and student, or to adjust her personality to make others comfortable in their own skin. She shouldn't have to compromise who she is to accommodate the insecurities of other girls her age, and yet so often, confident women dull their edge to prevent deflating another sister.

Rather than celebrating a success or sharing a promotion, we will quiet our accomplishments and maintain status quo so as not to upset others who may find our strength, education, or talent intimidating. This prevents us from fully entering into a sacred sisterhood where we can unapologetically be ourselves and share in the good things that are happening in our lives.

Naomi Torres-Mackie writes, "The subconscious, internalized message behind 'She's just jealous' can easily become: 'In order to not be threatening to other women, I must soften my presentation, diminish my accomplishments, downplay my assets.' Women are socialized to self-shrink in many areas, and the 'She's just jealous' refrain perpetuates that."[6]

We have learned to dim our shine rather than model to one another the power of our collective light.

She goes on to say, "On a macro level, 'She's just jealous' is another modern-day reinforcement of the idea that women are inherently against each other. It indicates that any social conflict among women can be explained by envy, or the idea that one woman's success results in another woman's resentment."

> We have learned to dim our shine rather than model to one another the power of our collective light.

When I became aware how easy it was to unintentionally communicate this idea that other girls were just jealous, I realized I was stunting my teen's growth in practicing healthy communication and conflict resolution. I want my daughter to remain true to who she is without the pressure of constantly thinking other girls see her as a threat. The only way to truly know why a friend had ghosted her, left her out, or said something catty was to be brave enough to ask her.

And not in a manipulative, whiny way, but with true curiosity as to why her friend was suddenly chilly or behaving differently.

When she began digging deeper and truly sought understanding, she usually discovered it wasn't jealousy that had caused a friend or teammate to act out. There were often extenuating circumstances such as family problems, pressure to perform, issues with a boy, a parent who was ill, or something else fueling her emotions. My daughter was just getting caught in the crossfire.

Once she realized this other girl was struggling with things that actually had nothing directly to do with her, she could pray for her, be a listening ear, and do her best to be a good friend to that person without feeling as if she needed to compromise herself. It began to rewrite her internal dialogue from defaulting to the assumption that behavior change in a friend always had to do with her.

When a fellow sister comes to you worried that another woman is acting strange or seemingly disconnected from them, do your best not to respond with "she's just jealous ..." and instead sit with your friend in the awkward tension of her situation. The empathy of letting her know she isn't alone, with the assurance that you are there for her as she navigates how and when to have a difficult conversation for clarity, is a great way to be a sacred sister.

When we encourage one another to do hard things and pursue each other in love, no matter how uncomfortable, this is iron sharpening iron. In the end, we all win as we extend to one another the same grace we hope to be given on a day we might act like a jealous friend.

We give to one another as freely as we have received from our Father.

Rewrite the Script

When it came to the complicated relationship between Cain and Abel, the scripture in Hebrews goes on to say, "It was what he *believed*, not what he *brought*, that made the difference. That's what God noticed and approved as righteous. After all these centuries, that belief continues to catch our notice" (11:4 MSG).

So often we allow jealousy of what others have or what they've been given, perceived stolen opportunities, to pervert the purity of true brotherhood and sisterhood. In reality, we're jealous of their faith and supposed favor, the enemy once again tricking us into coveting what others have rather than entering into a covenant with one another as sisters in Christ.

We have a jealous God who loves us with an *agape*, or the highest form of love, that never dies or grows cold. He offers us love regardless of our behavior, our desire to spend time with him, or how often we talk to him. He wants all of us: all our worship and praise and gratitude. In his perfect jealous love, he pursues us, even in our sin and wrongdoing. He never stops chasing us, looking for us when we wander off and celebrating when we return.

In John 13:34–35, Jesus gives us a very specific command:

"So now I am giving you a new commandment: Love each other. Just as I have loved you, you should love each other. Your love for one another will prove to the world that you are my disciples."

Agape love is the opposite of jealousy.

When we as the daughters of God offer to another this selfless form of love, we are modeling what it looks like to follow Jesus.

Romans 12:9–10 in *The Message* lays it out: "Love from the center of who you are; don't fake it. Run for dear life from evil; hold on for dear life to good. Be good friends who love deeply; practice playing second fiddle."

Sisters, we are to prefer one another.

What does it mean to prefer one another?

Paul writes this: "It is absolutely clear that God has called you to a free life. Just make sure that you don't use this freedom as an excuse to do whatever you want to do and destroy your freedom. Rather, *use your freedom to serve one another in love*; that's how freedom grows. For everything we know about God's Word is summed up in a single sentence: *Love others as you love yourself.* That's an act of true freedom. If you bite and ravage each other, watch out—in no time at all you will be annihilating each other, and where will your precious freedom be then?" (Gal. 5:13–15 MSG).

The entire chapter of Galatians 5 is convicting, but how it ends leaves me wanting to be the kind of friend who walks in freedom in this agape love Jesus has modeled to us.

He ends with verses 25 and 26 instructing, "Since this is the kind of life we have chosen, the life of the Spirit, let us make sure that we do not just hold it as an idea in our heads or a sentiment in our hearts, but work out its implications in every detail of our lives. *That means we will not compare ourselves with each other as if one of us were better and another worse.* We have far more interesting things to do with our lives. *Each of us is an original*" (MSG).

If we are to live a life of freedom, without jealousy and envy, we are to show the same love to one another as Christ offers to us.

In the fall of 2024, my second book released into the world. I was working a conference in Orlando, and it felt anticlimactic compared to my first book. I had bunked with a friend and her sister in their hotel room, and I woke up on the release date feeling a bit bummed. I hopped in the shower to prepare for the day, and when I emerged, I found a gift on my bed, flowers on the nightstand, and two sisters sitting on the edge of the bed grinning from ear to ear.

"Happy release day!" they shouted, hugging me and giggling as I unwrapped the glittering wrapping paper, holding back tears of shock and much-needed joy. The box was filled with special trinkets and a card reminding me that what I had just brought into the world was worth celebrating. I didn't expect it; I wasn't owed a party or celebration, but the fact that they took the time to pack a gift for me in their luggage from Nashville to Orlando spoke volumes. Their agape love wrapped around me and reminded me I wasn't in this alone.

Sacred sisterhood is intentional and sacrificial.

Jealousy throws shade.

Love throws confetti.

Flip Your Script

1. Have you ever been jealous of someone? How did it make you feel?

2. When you look into the lives of other women, what is it they have that you wish you had? Is there a common theme in your life (money, status, size of house, material things, work) that triggers you more than others?

3. What are some steps you can take to prevent jealousy from creeping in? Perhaps it's unfollowing certain people on social media or confessing you are jealous of a good friend or family member. Take time daily to count each of your blessings; God is generous to each of his daughters.

Chapter 6

"Women Are So Emotional ..."

"There's no crying in baseball."

Tom Hanks, *A League of Their Own*

I'm standing at the back of the room, the same room where just two years ago I was hanging in the doorway begging God not to make me go in, but now I'm inviting others in as the music swells for the final night of our women's ministry spring semester.

Hundreds of women have spread out in the room and are making their way from station to station kneeling, worshipping, praying with one another, taking part in journaling activities, nailing their sins to the cross, lighting candles for their unsaved friends and family. I am in awe of all God has done in the last two years: bringing us through a pandemic and a leadership transition that led me from the associate role to now full-time women's pastor.

With the help of other pastors on our staff and invested volunteers, we changed our format for women's ministry to create more opportunities for women to lead and serve one another. I can see now that my team is a gift from God, the women who have stepped into leadership roles the real MVPs, and I find myself humbled that I have been entrusted to this space despite my earlier temper tantrums and pity parties on my office floor.

"Pastor Natalie?"

I turn around to see a dear lady who has become a sweet friend the last two years. She's been through a lot and we've stayed close, even when we were confined to meeting online to pray her through a cancer scare and other medical issues that have left her frail but still hopeful.

I gently reach around her slender shoulders and pull her in close. I ask her how she is, how she is feeling as we stand in the darkness near the wooden cross. Even in the shadows, I can tell something is wrong, and with a quivering lip she simply replies, "The cancer is back."

In that moment I'm not strong like a pastor should be strong, or prophetic like a prophet is supposed to be. I'm not encouraging or optimistic, courageous or resilient. As she leans her stooped shoulders into me, I hold her up, and we sob loud cries to our Father who is familiar with our tears. We stand there for a long time as some gather around us in solidarity, and others graciously move on to make space for the moment.

Because sometimes worship and wailing sound the same.

There's No Crying in ...

In the 1992 film *A League of Their Own*, there was one line in the script that would stick with moviegoers for generations to come. "There's no crying in baseball."

The movie was set in World War II when most men were off fighting in the war and most of the jobs left vacant by their absence were filled by women, including some team sports. Not wanting baseball to die out, the owners decided to form new teams consisting of female players.

In an infamous scene, the coach of the Rockford Peaches, played by actor Tom Hanks, yells at one of his female players for ruining a play. As he gets louder and more aggressive, modeling how he had been coached as a player, she begins to break down into tears, which leads us to the iconic moment in the film where the coach loudly responds with disdain, "There's no crying in baseball!"

The umpire, seeing the commotion and tears in the dugout, addresses the agitated coach, "Perhaps you chastised her too vehemently. Good rule of thumb, you treat each of these girls as you'd treat your mother."

Though I have never played on a professional women's baseball team with an overly aggressive male coach, I have found myself in male-dominated spaces both in the corporate world and in the church. Also sitting at these tables were women who had adapted to their environment, turning off their emotions to keep things strictly business, doing all they could to ensure they never lost their seat at the table.

I have witnessed moments of intense plays being made financially, emotionally, and spiritually in boardrooms and staff meetings where emotions and stakes were high. And as a woman, there have been times I have fought back tears as my male peers used their volume, position, and physical size to get decisions pushed through—decisions that weren't always wise or strategic. In those moments I convinced myself that my tears, though equally as passionate and important as their volume, would present me as weak.

Too often I have found myself a hostage to my emotions, oscillating between anger and frustration, immobilized, believing the lies:

"There's no crying in business."
"There's no crying in motherhood."
"There's no crying in ministry."

Emotions Are from God

In our Drama Queen chapter, we talked a lot about emotional intelligence and the importance of understanding how our presence can shift a room. Emotions are powerful with the potential to be explosive when not under submission to their Creator. God's Word teaches that self-control is a Fruit of the Spirit; this is true for us as women, and for our brothers as well.

But when I read the Scriptures, I see a lot of emotion:

In Genesis 6:6, God is grieved in his heart.

In John 11:35, Jesus weeps over the death of Lazarus.

In Genesis 4, Cain gives way to anger and jealousy, resulting in the murder of his own brother.

In 1 Samuel 28, Saul falls into depression when God rejects him as king.

And fear? God's people knew something about that. There are nearly seventy scriptures that tell us not to be afraid. God tells Joshua in Joshua 1:9, "This is my command—be strong and courageous! Do not be afraid or discouraged. For the LORD your God is with you wherever you go."

In John 18:10–11, Peter shows impulsiveness and anger: "Then Simon Peter drew a sword and slashed off the right ear of Malchus, the high priest's slave. But Jesus said to Peter, 'Put your sword back into its sheath. Shall I not drink from the cup of suffering the Father has given me?'" (v. 11).

Rather than scream into Peter's face, "There's no anger in the garden!" Jesus asks him to put away his sword and consider the will of God to be more powerful than revenge.

God isn't weary with our emotions, but he does want to teach us how to use them in ways that glorify him and those around us. His Word is full of wisdom in teaching us how to let the Holy Spirit guide us when our emotions are tempted to take over.

"A hot-tempered person starts fights; a cool-tempered person stops them" (Prov. 15:18).

"'Don't sin by letting anger control you.' Don't let the sun go down while you are still angry" (Eph. 4:26).

We're also told there will be seasons of emotions in Ecclesiastes chapter 3: "A time to cry and a time to laugh. A time to grieve and a time to dance" (v. 4).

As humans, God has given us tears, laughter, anger, grief ... not to be wielded against us or toward another but to bring empathy, hope, and joy to our humanity. We aren't robots. It's okay to feel, as long as our feelings don't overpower our faith.

God is teaching us that while feelings can be good, they can fail us, which is why we need the Holy Spirit to guide us when our emotions try to take the wheel.

And as women, God isn't asking us to emote like men. He made us tenderly, gently, passionately, and with great intentionality—in his image. He gave us everything we would need to mother the nations, nurture those entrusted to us, lead others, partner with our brothers, and model his nature unapologetically.

But we cannot ignore the end result of Eve's disobedience in the garden. In Genesis, God reveals a portion of the repercussions of her choice to eat from the forbidden tree in chapter 3 verse 16:

"Then he said to the woman, 'I will sharpen the pain of your pregnancy, and in pain you will give birth. And you will desire to control your husband, but he will rule over you.'"

With this would also come hormones and menstruation cycles unique to us as women that would affect each of us in different ways. Because of this, we often find ourselves working extra hard at self-regulation, self-control, and self-awareness, which can feel overwhelming and unfair, especially when there are both physical and spiritual factors at play.

Power Under Control

It was a beautiful, hot summer day on the beach, the Gulf of Mexico brilliantly green against the solid blue sky and the white sand nearly blinding for anyone not wearing sunglasses. My parents had brought my sister and me down to Siesta Key, Florida, for a weeklong beach trip before we headed back to college for the fall semester.

As I rested on my towel, soaking in the sunshine and scanning the perfectly calm sea, something caught my eye—far out by the sandbar where my dad liked to hunt for shells. I took my sunglasses off and squinted into the sparkling waters. I saw it again; it was a fin!

I jumped up and ran to the water's edge where kids were building sandcastles as their parents floated in bright rafts well beyond the buoys. I watched as snorkelers swam closer to the sandbar and looked over to the vacant lifeguard stands. My eyes darted back toward the water, and I saw it again: a gray fin cutting through the water like a knife. Without another thought in my head, I screamed at the top of my lungs.

"SHARK!"

You can imagine the chaos that followed. Lifeguards came from literally nowhere as adults frantically ran to grab their children from the shallow waters and those in rafts paddled furiously back to shore. Kids screamed as their shovels were carried out to sea with the tide, their moats filling with water. Paddleboarders reluctantly exited the ocean, dragging their ten-foot boards behind them.

I stood there as adrenaline pumped through my veins, waiting to be hailed a local hero for saving hundreds from the massive jaws of a great white shark.

Turns out, I didn't save anyone from Jaws; I saved them from Flipper.

My great white was actually a dolphin.

After a quick lesson on how to decipher a shark fin from a dolphin fin by a less-than-amused, underpaid lifeguard, I sat on my towel feeling a whole new set of emotions as the adrenaline faded, leaving my body like a wilted balloon.

I had good intentions. I wanted to help people and maybe even save their lives.

How easy it had been to let my emotions get the best of me and to use my voice, meant to bring order, to cause panic and confusion.

I was quiet the rest of that day and into the rest of our vacation, suddenly very aware of the power my voice carried and how often it took orders from my wild emotions rather than discernment and wisdom.

It brought up some of my old insecurities from being a little girl who was told she talked too much and laughed too loud. Was I too much? Would this be my lot in life: the loud girl? I had always heard that Christian women should be meek, and in my mind, I already felt disqualified. I was the opposite of meek. I wasn't quiet, I wasn't demure, I wasn't always mindful.

But as I studied that word in the Bible, I learned that meekness isn't weakness; it's power under control. I can accept all the power God has given me as his daughter—all the anointing, talents, and gifts—and use them to the strength that I feel directed by the Holy Spirit without clearing an entire beach.

I began to study Esther and observed her posture in the palace as she approached the king for the freedom of her people, the Jews. She knew their lives were in danger, she knew the plot of the wicked Haman to destroy the Jewish people, but rather than scream, "SHARK!" at the top of her lungs, she called all the Jewish women together to pray and fast alongside her as she sought the Lord for her next steps.

> As I studied that word in the Bible, I learned that meekness isn't weakness; it's power under control.

She knew going to the king at the wrong time could get her killed, so she couldn't let her emotions get the best of her.

Observing Queen Esther and other women in the faith who I admire operate in this meekness was a testament of how God will use us when we let him guide our emotions. I began watching how women sat in difficult meetings, hard conversations, and having their reputations questioned but remaining still and silent before the Lord. However, I also saw them allowing tears to fall, their voices to grow in both volume and conviction without ever losing control, bringing change and clarity through their raw emotion. I witnessed humility modeled firsthand and learned through mentorship and discipleship how to lead others with a heart for Jesus, not always a need for justice.

You, too, my sweet sister, host emotions that aren't wrong or disruptive. When used as power under control, your emotions can mature into God-given authority through the Holy Spirit that brings order and peace to those around you.

You aren't too emotional.

You are perfectly a woman.

When Anxiety Attacks

I can remember looking at my doctor several years ago and telling her, "I'm tired of the thoughts in my head that won't turn off." It had been a very difficult three years in full-time ministry, our family had moved over a thousand miles from our hometown, and I wasn't sleeping. My mind was constantly racing, my emotions were all over the map, and I was dealing with debilitating medical anxiety that made me feel as if death were at my door every moment of every day.

What if my children grew up without their mother?

What if my husband died of a heart attack?

What if one of my daughters went missing?

These intrusive thoughts left me googling all sorts of medical conditions late into the night as I attempted to self-diagnose, exhausting myself and my family and adding to the normal stress of life and my changes in hormones. Satan was fighting overtime on my body and brain.

I had grown up in a denomination where it was frowned upon to take any type of medication for mental health or go to a counselor—even a Christian one. It was believed the need for either of these meant you lacked faith in God as your healer, and this stigma had stuck with me, even as I watched members of my own family wrestle with anxiety and depression for years.

To finally sit with a Christian primary care physician and be assured I was normal and that with monitored professional care—in addition to medication, prayer, and surrounding myself with biblical community—I could find relief brought me to tears in her office.

I have seen friends struggle with perception and even guilt for needing mental health support through postpartum depression, seasons of deep grief, transition, change, hormones, and genetics. At times it felt like a secret society of the serotonin sisters, all of us looking for sunlight and protein to keep our spirits high and emotions at bay. It felt like a death sentence—worse than what we were already enduring—to risk admitting in professional spaces that we needed help, so we suffered in silence. Until we didn't keep silent any longer.

The lies of the enemy were loud and told us we were the only ones.

"If you really trusted Jesus, you wouldn't need that medication."

"A good mom can manage all this without it."

"See, this is why women shouldn't be in ministry."

I know these scripts ran through my head on repeat as I put my kids to sleep, heart pounding, thoughts racing, pins and needles sensations running up and down my body. Anxiety threatened to keep me up through the night only for me to pretend to be fine the next day.

I slept with a Bible under my pillow, quoting scriptures instead of counting sheep:

"Don't worry about anything; instead, pray about everything. Tell God what you need, and thank him for all he has done. Then you will experience God's peace, which exceeds anything we can understand. His peace will guard your hearts and minds as you live in Christ Jesus" (Phil. 4:6–7).

"For God has not given us a spirit of fear and timidity, but of power, love, and self-discipline" (2 Tim. 1:7).

"So don't worry about tomorrow, for tomorrow will bring its own worries. Today's trouble is enough for today" (Matt. 6:34).

"Don't be afraid, for I am with you. Don't be discouraged, for I am your God. I will strengthen you and help you. I will hold you up with my victorious right hand" (Isa. 41:10).

I played worship music 24/7 in my house and car, declaring God's Word in song and trusting him to bring me relief.

I did everything I could spiritually, and combined with the wisdom of doctors whom God provided to me in this very difficult season, I slowly came off all medication with time, counseling, and daily workouts.

I realize this might not be your story or your final outcome. For many, medications and biblical counseling will be part of a lifetime of healing as God shows up as your peace and protector, defender and advocate alongside medical professionals. But this I know:

God has given each of us a sound mind for a spirit of fear, and this is our inheritance: peace that passes all understanding, joy unspeakable and filled with his glory, hope in a God who never leaves us or forsakes us, and his promises that are yes and amen.

Our role as women is not to judge one another, or try to fix each other, but to sit in these sacred spaces with each other where we can share our struggles and find intercessors who will pray us through the night. Worship with us through the wailing, lament with us in our tears, and wait with us for our healing.

Are you still looking for sacred sisterhood? Just know that this lifetime commitment is one of unconditional love, patience, perseverance, and a deep conviction that no matter how hard life gets, we won't give up on each other.

> Our role as women is not to judge one another, or try to fix each other, but to sit in these sacred spaces with each other.

To quote Joy from the children's movie *Inside Out 2*, which has spoken loudly over many of us, I speak this over you ...

"You don't get to choose who Riley is. Anxiety, you need to let her go."[7]

And to the real enemy of our souls, I'll take it a step further ...

Satan, you don't get to steal the peace and joy from my sisters. In the name of Jesus, let her go.

Rewrite the Script

It has been my observation that women tend to be more patient with children and men than we are with one another. I first came to this startling revelation when I was pregnant with my first child. I started with two male doctors who were gentle and took their time with my questions and listened to my concerns. But then, halfway through my pregnancy, our new insurance forced me to change to another practice, and I found myself under the care of a female OB/GYN. I hoped that she would be equally, if not more, compassionate and patient.

What I found was quite the opposite. Our visits were quick and even cold at times, with her rushing in and dismissive of my inquiries. It was as if because we shared the same body parts, I should just know how to deliver a baby. Yes, I valued medical professionalism, but I also needed reassurance and even a little empathy, and this was another woman who had not only given birth to her own healthy babies, but delivered hundreds more.

Just as the umpire encouraged the male coach to treat his players like he would his own mother, I encourage us as sisters in Christ to treat one another with the same patience and kindness we would like to be shown. Just because we share the same anatomical parts doesn't mean we have all had the same life experiences. Just because we have similar hormones doesn't mean we share the same struggles or strongholds.

Yes, women can be emotional, and we can have overly emotional seasons in life, but that doesn't define who we are as daughters of God.

Please do not write off a sister in Christ because of how she responds in a difficult season.

I am so thankful for my sacred sisters who have stood by me in my grief, fear, irrational responses, failures, quietness, overbearingness, frustration, and selfishness. Their commitment to our friendship—holding me accountable when I forget how to self-regulate and operate in self-control—gently guides me back to the arms of my Father, even if I go kicking and screaming.

Even if it leads me to my doctor's office.

Even if it leads me to taking medication.

Even if it leads me into a counselor's office.

Because sacred sisters never leave us when we are hurting; rather, they walk us toward our healing.

Yes, women can be emotional.

We can also be so:

Affectionate
Joyful
Loving
Sympathetic
Hilarious
Encouraging
Sweet
Gentle
Wise
Kind

And, sisters, sometimes, there is crying in baseball.

Flip Your Script

1. What was your home like growing up? Did your parents show emotion? What were the responses when you showed emotion? How has that impacted your reactions to things in the present?

2. What emotions do you struggle to control in your life today? Is it anger, fear, anxiety, sadness? Who do you trust to share this with who can pray with you?

3. How do you respond to the emotions of other women? Are you patient and willing to sit with others in their suffering? Do you expect others to react in similar ways to you? Part of sacred sisterhood is bearing one another's burdens and staying with them even when we're ready to move on.

Chapter 7

"Women Are So Catty..."

> *"Be gracious in your speech. The goal is to bring out the best in others in a conversation, not put them down, not cut them out."*
>
> Colossians 4:5–6 MSG

The local Starbucks is hopping and I'm gingerly sipping on my sugar-free vanilla latte as my eyes scan the crowd, watching for my ten o'clock appointment. I'm dreading this conversation. Since taking on the full-time role of women's pastor, there have been so many beautiful moments and lessons learned. God has wrecked me in the gentlest ways, teaching me how to sit with women through grief, joy, frustration, disagreements, and today I would be learning the lesson of repentance.

You see, I spent the first year and a half as associate women's pastor throwing tantrums and living in survival mode. It was every woman for herself as our little team navigated unhealthy leadership and challenging relationships. I hadn't been a good friend or pastor to one of our women, who had been treated unfairly and then dismissed. I didn't defend her; in fact, I partnered with the toxicity to spare my job and survive.

I had used my words to defend myself but never to defend my sister. My silence spoke volumes.

For the past several weeks, the Lord has been dealing with me and I can't stop thinking about her. Last week I called her and today we are having coffee, and I don't know how it will go. Her identity, calling, and anointing were called into question, and as I've done healing work, it has become clear the Lord is convicting me to ask her for forgiveness in partnering with the abuse she endured.

She walks through the door and sits down at the table, her posture stiff but eyes kind. I assume she is waiting to get coffee to see what kind of meeting I have called her for, and I hate that she looks guarded.

I start quick and to the point. "I am so sorry for hurting you and partnering with the lies spoken over you through my silence and indifference. Please forgive me for every word, deed, interaction, and time I didn't defend you."

She looks at me with tears threatening to fall, but I can see her clenched jaw is calling them back into submission. She gets up with her purse, and I am ready to accept her rejection, but rather than run for the door, she goes to the barista to place her order.

We are both going to need coffee …

Catfight

Over the years, I've heard many reasons why women don't like each other, and "women are catty" always made the list. This one comes from women both inside and outside of the church, from Christ followers and those still on a journey to finding Jesus, so I knew we had to talk about it. I wasn't quite sure what the true definition of the term "catty" was, so I did a little research and quickly understood why this was a top contender for a chapter.

The term "catty" is predominantly used by women to describe the unhealthy way another woman responds to an otherwise healthy feeling of competition.

It's using our words in direct and indirect ways to be unpleasant or unkind with subtle hostility to hurt, annoy, or upset another individual—primarily women. This is where we get the term "catfight" that we often hear when describing a female confrontation or heated argument, possibly even a physical altercation.

Most of the time these remarks, meant to cause insecurity and other emotional reactions, are driven by competition and intended to hurt another without bringing physical harm to the offended.

The fact that "catty" was the honest term most women shot back to me when I asked what they had said about other women in the past speaks loudly. We have clearly used our words and rhetoric to hurt each other. And for what purpose?

Women of the church, I'm not mad; I'm disappointed. Because we know better, but we don't always do better, and we must do better. There's a spiritual epidemic and it's not just women leaving

> **Women of the church, I'm not mad; I'm disappointed. Because we know better, but we don't always do better.**

the church because they got hurt by another woman. No, women are giving up on the hopes of sacred sisterhood from lonely and broken hearts.

We make assumptions, assign motives, judge the past, and fail to see hope for another's future. We talk big behind closed doors and behind the backs of our sisters but refuse to acknowledge elephants in the room lest they reveal our own loneliness, insecurities, sin, or secrets. We assign scapegoats and put other women in straitjackets to protect our reputations and positions. We break one another down when we're called to build each other up, but I guess it is easier to blame another sister than to look in the mirror and own our part, how we have wounded others with our words and actions.

I've known and met too many who have been betrayed and then had their lives talked about and dissected by those they trusted, stood beside, cheered on, shared a pew with, and defended. It is less painful to be kicked by a stranger than kissed on the cheek by a betrayer. Jesus knows.

When the hurt happens on holy ground—at the hands of those who should be our sacred sisters—it is a soul-shaking sadness, a mind-numbing math problem without a solution. This heartbreaking, gut-wrenching pain that makes us want to puke can lead us to preach from our pulpits of social media.

We want justice one minute and we're too tired to contend for friendship the next. That doesn't make us difficult or indifferent, it makes us human, but God knows what to do with our humanity.

For those who have been hurt by women in the church, we need to know that our broken heart isn't our ending but is the beginning to opening our hearts to others who might be ready to give up. You're alive, you're still here, and yes, you've been ripped apart, but somehow you have managed to wear your wounds with great humility and strength. Other women are inspired by seeing our scars and hearing our stories of redemption that come with it.

I feel like that protective big sister in the family of God, and the more I hear your stories of being hurt by women in the church and reflect on my own stories, I realize how easy it is to say we're a hospital for the sick while poisoning our own water. The entire church, not just when women gather, should be a spring of Living Water that restores, redeems, and heals through the biblical community we see modeled by Jesus throughout the Scriptures.

Paul encourages us in Colossians to "use your heads as you live and work among outsiders. Don't miss a trick. Make the most of every opportunity. Be gracious in your speech. The goal is to bring out the best in others in a conversation, not put them down, not cut them out" (4:5–6 MSG).

Healing Honey for Sticks and Stones

I remember hearing as a child "sticks and stones can break my bones, but words can never hurt me" and thinking how ridiculous that was. Not only could words hurt me, they could actually bring death—figuratively and literally.

Scripture tells us, "The good person out of the good treasure of his heart produces good, and the evil person out of his evil treasure produces evil, for out of the abundance of the heart his mouth speaks" (Luke 6:45 ESV).

It also says,

"Don't use foul or abusive language. Let everything you say be good and helpful, so that your words will be an encouragement to those who hear them" (Eph. 4:29).

As Christians, we should ooze words of life in every conversation and interaction, whether with our sisters in Christ or those we meet in everyday life. Yet what I'm hearing from women in the church is that we have a long way to go. We aren't building tables; we're putting up fences. We aren't pulling up chairs; we're being exclusive and surrounding ourselves with women who look like us and talk like us. We aren't being prophetic; we're being pathetic in our attempt to stay queen bee in a hive that is no longer producing honey.

"Women do compete, and they can compete quite fiercely with one another," said Tracy Vaillancourt, a psychology professor at the University of Ottawa in Canada. "The form it typically takes is indirect aggression, because it has a low cost: The person [making the attack] doesn't get injured. Oftentimes, the person's motives aren't detected, and yet it still inflicts harm against the person they're aggressing against."[8]

From my personal experience, I have found that a woman being catty is less about being a woman and more about a desire for power and control, two things women like to have but don't always know how to manage in healthy ways.

When we say, "women are so catty," it is most likely because we have experienced a woman or women in our lives who have wanted to knock us down a few notches to validate their own position or dominance. We might have been simple bystanders who somehow found our way into their path, or we might have had the unfortunate reality of working for them or with them every day. It could have been a friend who was feeling jealous or as if they were losing control in a certain area of their life, or even a stranger at the airport who was having a bad day.

We use our words, directly and indirectly, to make a point and let people know where they stand, and it can be divisive, harmful, and dehumanizing to those in our wake. In a nutshell, it is sin.

James doesn't mince any words in warning us of the importance of using our words to speak life. He writes in James chapter 3:

> A bit in the mouth of a horse controls the whole horse. A small rudder on a huge ship in the hands of a skilled captain sets a course in the face of the strongest winds. A word out of your mouth may seem of no account, but it can accomplish nearly anything—or destroy it! It only takes a spark, remember, to set off a forest fire. A careless or wrongly placed word out of your mouth can do that. By our speech we can ruin the world, turn

> harmony to chaos, throw mud on a reputation, send the whole world up in smoke and go up in smoke with it, smoke right from the pit of hell. (vv. 3–6 MSG)

But wait, he isn't finished yet ...

> This is scary: You can tame a tiger, but you can't tame a tongue—it's never been done. The tongue runs wild, a wanton killer. With our tongues we bless God our Father; with the same tongues we curse the very men and women he made in his image. Curses and blessings out of the same mouth! My friends, this can't go on. A spring doesn't gush fresh water one day and brackish the next, does it? Apple trees don't bear strawberries, do they? Raspberry bushes don't bear apples, do they? You're not going to dip into a polluted mud hole and get a cup of clear, cool water, are you? (vv. 7–12 MSG)

We could write an entire Bible study off this passage alone to bring clarity to this catty conversation.

But here is what I know: catty behavior doesn't belong in the church.

When I took my poll to social media platforms and asked women what they wanted to talk about on this subject, the consensus was clear: we've all been wounded by catty women. Yet what wasn't as obvious was taking ownership of our own catty behavior—because, ladies, we all have claws.

Writing this book has convicted me to look deep within my own heart for any wickedness that might lie within me. Where have I used words to indirectly cut others down? When have I been competitive or my own thoughts turned bitter and unkind toward another sister?

The Scriptures are clear: "And I tell you this, you must give an account on judgment day for every idle word you speak" (Matt. 12:36).

That word "idle" means to lack worth or any real basis. It's blowing hot air to puff up our own pride. It's speaking without placing weight on our words. The idle words we speak toward and over our sisters lack value and life, essentially placing words of death over them that steal from the treasure within them.

Women are intelligent. We know when we're being talked down to, spoken poorly of, being dismissed or disregarded. So when we walk into a church, a small group, a Bible study, or a women's event and we sense one ounce of catty behavior, it will most likely be the last time we attempt to step back into that community, or possibly any community of women.

We already have to deal with competition, jealousy, and malice in the world; the women of the church should be modeling the opposite. We shouldn't be the ones opening old wounds or creating new ones. Our words should sing life over broken hearts and soothe those wounded by the world.

As daughters of God, when other women walk through our church doors, into our small group, or sit down at a women's gathering, we should make them feel so special, so wanted, so adored that they leave feeling ten feet tall. We should leave every sister better than we found her.

As Christian women, we should constantly be scouring our local grocery store, doctor's office, gym, and children's schools for other women who may not call Jesus Lord of their life just yet to encourage and speak life over. They are watching us; they want to know if we're different or if we're just the PG version of the mean girls of the world.

How's Your Fruit?

In the first church of Acts, the Scriptures tell us that people from the outside looking into the upper room "in general liked what they saw" (2:47 MSG).

What did they like? Well, it could have been the tongues of fire and Holy Spirit encounter, but I think it was more. The church was being added to daily but not just because the people had charisma and gifts, which 1 Corinthians 12:8–10 mentions as wisdom, knowledge, faith, healing, miracles, prophecy, discerning of spirits, speaking in tongues, and the interpretation of tongues. I believe it's because they witnessed salvation, repentance, worship, communion, breaking of bread, and other elements that made them stop and look into the windows with curiosity.

They saw what Galatians describes as the fruit:

- love
- joy
- peace
- forbearance
- kindness
- goodness
- faithfulness
- gentleness
- self-control

There were women included in that upper room, and the proof was in the fruit of those who went out and took the message of Jesus Christ to the ends of the earth. Gifts are great; they are an overflow of our time spent with Jesus and his Word as we allow him to convict us, grow us, and change us for his glory and our good. Gifts such as teaching, preaching, prophecy, wisdom, service, and administration—the many gifts that women in the church have today—are beautiful and needed, but fruit takes root when placed in healthy soil. If the fruit is there, the gifts will follow.

If we want our ministries to grow, our churches to expand, for the Great Commission to reach far and wide, we have to resolve right now that we will be women who grow good fruit so others find Jesus through every interaction with us.

Some of our ministries and endeavors might not be growing because we're mean. We're catty. Competitive. Opportunistic. Lazy, complacent. Jealous. Discontent. Impatient. Looking for coattails to ride rather than new territory to plow.

When God gives us something, when he entrusts us with his people, he will require a level of maturity and responsibility. He won't elevate bullies or anoint self-appointed kings. If your ministry isn't growing, if you have a hard time finding sacred sisters, check your soil. If there isn't any fruit, it might be because you aren't connected to the vine: Jesus.

As the Lord has expanded my vineyard around the world, I have learned the value of good fruit as I meet team members, volunteers, staff, and congregants giving their time to serve their churches and pastors. With each interaction, I am convicted to speak to each individual as if they could be the senior pastor because, as a child of God, every person deserves to be spoken to with respect and care.

> **If your ministry isn't growing, if you have a hard time finding sacred sisters, check your soil.**

Early in ministry, I begged God to show me fruit (proof) he was in my endeavors. I thought the fruit was open doors, opportunities, and relationships, but I was quick to find I lacked fruit in some areas.

God always cares how we treat and speak to each other. If we use people for stepping stones or doormats, he certainly won't give us more ground to walk. If we're angry, combative, frustrated, or jealous of the success of others while we're trying to build something pure, it won't last.

If God has given you a vision or a ministry idea or anything to use for him, he will always add the great command to that mission: loving God and loving people. When we follow that, we will build the Kingdom with God through what we've been given rather than shifting man-made castles on flimsy foundations.

People aren't for getting us where we want to be.

People are the priority, and Jesus is the prize.

Rewrite the Script

If our words have the power to either give life or bring death, this means many women are walking around fully alive or on their deathbed. As sisters in Christ, we have the opportunity to break the word curses that have been placed on us, using words that bless and encourage.

But we need to change how we speak of and to other women, and it's clear we as women in the church have some healing work to do.

Synonyms for "catty" are pretty intense. They include:

- rancorous
- spiteful
- evil
- mean
- backbiting
- hateful
- ill-natured
- malevolent
- venomous
- vicious
- wicked

And the antonyms? They are quite simple:

- loving
- benevolent

- sympathetic
- compassionate
- gracious
- good
- kind

This sounds a lot like Jesus.

Together, we can agree we won't be Christian divas. We won't let our titles or positions keep us from forming friendships with those who don't carry the same credentials.

We won't treat women in leadership differently than we treat our friends who aren't in leadership.

We won't demand to be treated differently because of who our parents are or who we have married.

We will respect one another as fellow sisters in Christ regardless of status.

Deep down, we all long to form a sacred sisterhood, but it will take each of us choosing to put aside our own insecurities—the need for popularity or approval—and meet each other right where we are. We need to choose to tear down our own walls so others won't be afraid to do the same.

How do we do this when we are working through our own issues with women, when we are trying to find our own seat at the table or deal with our fears of rejection?

The answer might surprise you: simply be nice.

When attending an event at your church or community, be the one to cross the room and say hello to a woman who looks lost or alone.

Be willing to go on the school field trip and talk to the other moms, even if they all seem to know each other.

Invite women into your home for a holiday event or to celebrate the first day of school. Celebrate them with a small gift as simple as a card with a Bible verse, a flower, their favorite candy, or a gift card to a coffee bar.

Send a card to another woman just because you were thinking of her.

Send a text saying you are praying for her.

And if all of this just seems like too much, a simple smile at another sister from across the room or telling her you love her shoes can go further than you will ever imagine.

My prayer for us, dear sisters, is that we would take every word spoken against us and replace them by releasing two more words of blessing over the women who come into our lives. Let us, the daughters of God, set the standard. Let us set it so high that everyone who comes into our presence, into our ministries, into our churches has no choice but to gladly rise to the occasion. I pray we try to outdo each other in love, peace, patience, joy ... one word, one woman at a time.

Flip Your Script

1. Have you ever asked someone to forgive you for something you've said or done? What was the response?

2. What are some healthy ways we can confront and shift catty behavior we see around us? Perhaps it's modeling generosity to one another in our words and in other ways, being the change we are desperate to see in our work environments, book clubs, church gatherings.

3. Have you had to forgive another woman? I encourage you to do that today, even if you never see her again or talk to her again, so you are free from the past and the pain.

Chapter 8

"Women Are So Controlling ..."

> "Better to be patient than powerful; better
> to have self-control than conquer a city."
>
> Proverbs 16:32

I'm staring at the fifty-six emails on my computer that I've read but marked as unread because I can only handle dealing with one or two at a time. With each new semester of the women's ministry calendar comes an influx of "suggestions" from women that sound more like complaints.

"Wednesday mornings would work better for most women ..."

"Could the worship be a little shorter?"

"I want to teach my own curriculum—why does the material have to be approved by the pastoral staff?"

"I need childcare on Thursday nights, not Tuesday nights ..."

My people-pleasing tendencies are in conflict with my impatience with women and their demands that make me feel more like a concierge service than a pastor. With every event, date, process, and procedure come suggestions in the form of personal preferences, and I realize we will never please everyone, though I try very hard.

I close my laptop and squeeze my eyes shut, committing to responding to two more of these requests tomorrow morning when I've had more time to pray.

Calling Out Control

When I was in high school, I really wanted to attend a certain party, but I knew my mom would never agree to let me go. I remember standing in the bathroom with her as she was getting ready ... saying all the right things, making all the right promises, using every trick I had up my sleeve to convince her as she silently let me plead my case. After several minutes she spun around, put her finger in my face, and said, "I will not raise a manipulative little girl!" then left me speechless and alone.

She knew I was trying to control her with manipulation for my own benefit, to get her to say yes to something I knew was a "no" for several reasons. She wasn't going to let me get away with it at fifteen years old because she knew something then that I hadn't learned: manipulative teenage girls can easily become manipulative women.

And manipulative women can often find themselves in positions in the local church where they are trusted to lead other women, resulting in this common phrase said among sisters: "Women are so controlling."

Dethroning Jezebel

I'm just going to come out and say it. We have got to stop labeling women who struggle with control as "Jezebel" when they do or say something that rubs us the wrong way.

The real Jezebel in the Bible makes her debut in 1 Kings 16, when King Ahab married her to assist in leading Israel into Baal worship. She was cunning, even controlling, as we see in 1 Kings 18 when she demands all the prophets of the Lord be killed. She went after Elijah the prophet and later Elisha; schemed with her husband, Ahab; and had another man, Naboth, killed to take his vineyard that he refused to sell to them out of obedience to God.

Jezebel suffers a gruesome, Old Testament death worthy of its own Netflix episode when she is thrown from a window and trampled by a horse after taunting Elisha. When they went to find her body, it had been eaten by dogs. No more Jezebel.

During her disastrous reign, Jezebel gained influence by saying all the right things, repeating prophetic declarations, and appointing herself as a prophet. You might be reading this and thinking you would *never* behave this way or call yourself a prophet, but it is easy to repeat Scripture and sound holy when attempting to persuade—or manipulate—others for personal benefit.

How do we know when we've gone from persuasive to manipulative?

- We use Scripture—to justify bad behavior or make others do what we want them to do.
- We hurt others in an attempt to save ourselves.

- We lie and deceive to cover our own sin.
- We feel no remorse when the consequence of our action affects others negatively.
- We believe processes and procedures put in place by leadership don't apply to us.
- We stop praying and seeking the wisdom of God through his Word and rely on our own desires and feelings.

Personally struggling with these things—or encountering someone in our churches or ministries who does—doesn't mean we have a "Jezebel Spirit" (as I've heard someone called), but it could indicate an issue with control that can lead us to sin and hurt others.

When I became a women's pastor, I didn't realize how many hours I would spend mediating conversations between women who were in conflict with one another. It never failed: as emotions took over, one woman would accuse the other woman of having the "Jezebel Spirit," and from there someone would either storm out of the room or we entered daytime-talk-show-level drama.

This accusation feels like low-hanging fruit, like little girls on a playground going for the jugular with the one insult they know will silence their foe. It is important for women to understand that just because another woman exhibits leadership or personality styles that carry power and grit and might feel intimidating doesn't mean they have a Jezebel Spirit. I have heard this too often—among multiple denominations—describing those from the platform to the pew, and it has to stop. It is a serious accusation that we will all be held accountable for wielding should it prove untrue.

In God's mercy, he will send us someone (like my mom) to call us out and rebuke our manipulative ways, to make us aware of our sinful natures so we can prayerfully repent.

> **Just because another woman exhibits leadership or personality styles that might feel intimidating doesn't mean they have a Jezebel Spirit.**

We should have tender hearts and be receptive if these people bravely come to us. This doesn't make us Jezebels, but it might mean we need to prayerfully take a step back, repent for how we have hurt others in our attempt to control (no matter how well-intentioned), and sit under biblical discipleship to help us heal and grow.

When we refuse to listen to those who are trying to help us, it becomes a dangerous situation for those we lead and for our own relationship with God.

The Many Faces of Control

I used to think I didn't have an issue with control until I found myself in situations where things weren't going the way I planned. I always considered myself along for the ride, until I realized I was white-knuckling my life, riding the clutch hard and grabbing for the steering wheel anytime God took me in a direction that wasn't on the GPS.

For younger Natalie, control looked like having perfect grades, wearing intricately curated outfits, getting into every school club, appearing to have it all together, writing down every morsel of food that went into my mouth, and making sure I was always at the best events. The older I got, the better I became at masking it as "excellence," "stewardship," or "responsibility."

If we go back to the beginning pages where we started this journey, sitting in that office where I was being told my job was changing from worship ministry to women's ministry, I was a woman who had lost all control. My family had moved over a thousand miles away from everyone and everything we knew, my husband had quit his very successful job, my children had left their schools and close friends, I had left my hometown where I'd spent thirty-seven years—all for this job. It felt as if everything were at stake.

My job.

My reputation.

My family.

My future.

Our future as a family.

The variety of emotions coursing through my body in that one singular moment, and my response, could result in a peaceful transition from one department to another or my termination of employment. I had no choice but to let go of the steering wheel and give God control, as I had done many times before, but this time it felt like it was costing me much more.

My identity.

My calling.

My creativity.

My position.

Turns out, I am a certified control freak, and when I feel as if I am losing control, my fallen self begins to rear its ugly head. I become that woman we all say we don't like: jealous, competitive, catty, emotional. I forget who I am and whose I am, and I become desperate, grabbing at all the buttons and knobs around me in the form of social media, position, status, and followers to try and make sense of the chaos.

When I reluctantly accepted my new role of women's pastor, life was a whirlwind of signing a new job description and moving my office from a place of creativity and community to a dark hallway set far away from most of the church staff. It didn't feel like a promotion. It didn't feel like leadership saw that I had a teaching gift. It felt as if I were being punished.

I couldn't control where my new office would be located, how the news of my new position would be communicated to the staff, how I would be perceived, and if others were creating their own narratives. I felt far away, isolated, and if I'm honest, forgotten some days when I looked out at the empty hall.

Word slowly trickled out and I began getting visitors during the day from other staff members and women I was meeting through my new role. They would bring coffee and snacks, and before I knew it, my little office became a safe haven for women to share life. We would pray, laugh, and cry in that quiet hallway set apart from the crazy world outside.

That office that previously felt like a punishment became my palm tree as I obediently stayed in a place I didn't want to be but had been called to serve, meeting with the people of God and speaking the Word of God over them.

Women, when we give God control, he can use us in ways we cannot even begin to imagine!

We see this modeled for us in the life of Deborah, who knew exactly who she was and didn't have to overthrow a kingdom or emasculate a brother to sit in her position as judge. Let's get to know a sacred sister in the faith:

> Deborah was a prophet, the wife of Lappidoth. She was judge over Israel at that time. She held court under Deborah's Palm between Ramah and Bethel in the hills of Ephraim. The People of Israel went to her in matters of justice.
>
> She sent for Barak son of Abinoam from Kedesh in Naphtali and said to him, "It has become clear that GOD, the God of Israel, commands you: Go to Mount Tabor and prepare for battle. Take ten companies of soldiers from Naphtali and Zebulun. I'll take care of getting Sisera, the leader of Jabin's army, to the Kishon River with all his chariots and troops. And I'll make sure you win the battle." (Judg. 4:4–7 MSG)

Here is what we know about Deborah:

- She was close in her relationship with God.
- She was a prophet—given divine knowledge through the Holy Spirit.
- She was wise—hearing from God and seeing in visions given to her from God.
- She was a servant to Israel and its people.
- She judged Israel in their time of oppression, not as if she were better than them but as a prophet who delivered the word of God.
- She corrected abusive behavior and listened to grievances.
- She was trusted to provide judgment, not just for quarrels between people but for advice and spiritual direction.
- She prayed for people, on their behalf to God.

Deborah ruled not from a place of control, but power under the control of the Holy Spirit. The people of Israel were under the oppression of Jabin, and God told Deborah to find Barak and instruct him to raise an army, giving him exact instructions on the number of soldiers he should gather and where they should go. Barak was to engage Jabin's forces that were under Sisera's command, but Barak hesitated.

Deborah was prepared to send Barak out to do the job he was trained to do, but he hesitated at her instructions.

He told her, "'If you go with me, I'll go. But if you don't go with me, I won't go.' She said, 'Of course I'll go with you. But understand that with an attitude like that, there'll be no glory in it for you. God will use a woman's hand to take care of Sisera'" (vv. 8–10 MSG).

Barak knew Deborah heard from God, so her presence assured him that God was with him as well. She wasn't trying to usurp his authority to steal his thunder. She went with him as a sacred sister who would provide counsel, wisdom, and strategy from God. She didn't control the mission, but she had so much confidence in Barak and in their God that she called his mission a "journey," not war.

She wasn't controlling; Deborah was confident in her God, strong in her faith, and walked in supernatural courage.

There is another woman in this story: Jael, the wife of Heber the Kenite who was friends with Jabin, king of Hazor. When the battle grew tense and Sisera came to her tent looking for a place of refuge, Jael stepped out to meet Sisera and said, "Come in, sir. Stay here with me. Don't be afraid" (v. 18 MSG).

The Scriptures tell us, "Then while he was fast asleep from exhaustion, Jael wife of Heber took a tent peg and hammer, tiptoed toward him, and drove the tent peg through his temple and all the way into the ground. He convulsed and died.

"Barak arrived in pursuit of Sisera. Jael went out to greet him. She said, 'Come, I'll show you the man you're looking for.' He went with her and there he was—Sisera, stretched out, dead, with a tent peg through his temple" (vv. 21–22 MSG).

Just as Deborah prophesied, God used a woman's hand to take out Sisera. From there, God subdued Jabin, king of Canaan, before the people of Israel.

Jael modeled a steady hand in a time of fear. How many times in her life, in moving her tent from place to place, had she removed a tent peg only to drive it back into the earth to secure their home in a new location? She had practiced this one action time and time again without realizing this muscle memory would come in handy when the enemy lay sleeping on her floor.

God didn't give Deborah or Jael opportunity in order to control the situation or one another. No, God used these two women to partner with others in freeing the people of Israel, and they did it together—not in competition but in collaboration.

We don't have to completely control the situation to prove we are strong, capable, or called. We just need to be looking for how God wants us to be obedient.

Simply being who God created us to be—positioned at our post with a tent peg in hand, ready to partner with our Kingdom brothers and sisters—can take our enemy down.

Can you imagine if Jael had hesitated in fear of stepping on Barak's toes? If she wasn't obedient to take advantage of a sleeping Sisera all because she didn't want to look like she was taking control or overstepping her role to Deborah?

Can you imagine if Jael was intimidated by Deborah and didn't want to appear in competition with her or taking her glory?

The difference is, every single day we as women forfeit our God-given authority to make both our brothers and sisters more comfortable, and the sleeping enemy wakes up to wreak havoc on the people of God once more.

Our fear of appearing controlling cannot be greater than our call to be obedient to the Lord.

> **Our fear of appearing controlling cannot be greater than our call to be obedient to the Lord.**

However, this can be easier said than done after a lifetime of being told we need to "stay in our lane" or being accused of being on a power trip simply for exercising the authority given to us.

Sometimes godly authority can appear threatening to men and women who haven't been manning their positions in the family of God.

If God has willing and capable daughters ready for war, he will use women to accomplish his work, and not as a backup plan but as his plan A.

Sister, if you find yourself grabbing the steering wheel for control or shrinking back so as not to rock the boat, rest in this:

- You don't need verbal recognition, but it's right to long for vocational respect. A handshake and an eye-to-eye "I'm proud of you" or "thank you" goes much further than public affirmation.
- We don't have to become more masculine to be accepted or more feminine to fit into someone's personal conviction of where women belong. We can be ourselves. We can have different hobbies and interests than our

- male counterparts and still be included in conversations and offer wisdom in areas of our specialty.
- You are not a trap to be avoided or a temptation to be feared. You can be confident in who you are in Christ without demanding validation or promotion as proof. You can walk in your prophetic calling without a corner office or time on the platform. Just be obedient and ask God for your next steps.

Don't pine for a seat at the table; build new tables with more elbow room. In fact, start constructing them in spaces that are barren. We all come with unique perspectives and life experiences. We carry discernment, wisdom, and fear of the Lord that can shed light on different areas of the church that the enemy has tried to keep in the dark.

We are the intercessors and greatest defenders. We work hard and we aren't afraid of frontline battle, but it feels lonely at times and we can grow weary of the constant warfare as we're attacked from within about trivial matters such as whose job it should be to do what we're all called to do: love God and one another.

But count it a joy to serve the people of God, your family, your friends. You are more than a sidekick to your boss or husband, more than a mascot for the Kingdom of God. The church needs what God has given you, and you will steward it well.

Don't quench the Holy Spirit by letting the enemy stop you from being used by God.

He knows his days are numbered when you are faithful to remain in position and obedient in your mission.

Grab a tent peg, sisters. This is war.

Rewrite the Script

If Deborah were to get a report card, I imagine the comment section might say "talks too much," "bossy with her friends," but it would be that potential, some describing her as a controlling and strong-willed little girl, that would one day set her under her palm tree where she would judge the people of Israel with confidence and authority given by God.

If Jael were in the same class, her comment section might say "gets a little rough with the boys at recess," and she may have gotten an A+ in gym class for her accuracy in archery. But it would be her tenacity and laser-sharp focus that would free a nation from an oppressor.

We have no idea why God gives us certain personality traits and asks us to walk out difficult scenarios in life. Where someone might interpret our holy chutzpah as domineering, God uses it for his glory because that's just what he does.

When Deborah told Barak that she would join him and warned him that victory would be at the hands of a woman, he didn't take offense. He welcomed Deborah because he knew she heard from God. He was willing to defer credit for the fall of Sisera, and in my opinion, that is what makes him a hero in this story. He didn't let his pride get in the way.

But, women, if there is a controlling bone in your body, put it under the submission and subjection of Christ and church leadership. Satan would like nothing more than to ruin our witness by using us as pawns in power plays.

In the church, the role of women in our pulpits and platforms has been a huge distraction that has led to denominational debate and division. While we've been taking votes in primarily male-dominated rooms as to who gets a voice, flipping TV trays over traditions, and tripping over egos, the enemy has been delighting in his every small victory along the way.

He doesn't need to sneak into our houses—we have left the front doors wide open. Innocence has been lost at the very hands who were supposed to protect it. While we have been sitting in rooms debating and fearing a woman might overstep or get too loud—too controlling—victims have been suffering in silence. Sadly, I have learned some are willing to offer a sacrifice of other lives if it means they win their religious war.

God is more worried about his sheep being protected than the gender of those leading his sheep.

God will raise up Deborahs to help lead his church and strike down Jezebels who have come to bring chaos and confusion. It is vital that we as his daughters are wise as serpents and gentle as doves in discerning those who have been given godly authority and prophetic wisdom versus those who simply know how to make something sound and look good to gain influence.

Look within your own soul and ask God to prune anything that isn't of him. If you're looking for Scripture to guide you in this prayer, sit with John and ask God to do the tedious work or remove anything that is keeping you from producing good fruit in your life, particularly in your friendship with women. John 15:2 tells us, "He cuts off every branch of mine that doesn't produce fruit, and he prunes the branches that do bear fruit so they will produce even more."

Then sit confidently under the palm tree where he has seated you with the tools he has placed in your hand. Exercise your authority, not your control.

Flip Your Script

1. What situations are you trying to control at the moment?

2. Who are you attempting to control? Is it a teen daughter, a coworker, a friend?

3. What is something God has told you to do that you haven't out of fear you will either miss out on another opportunity or fail? What palm tree have you abandoned or what tent peg are you refusing to pick up in your attempt to control the outcome?

Chapter 9

"Women Are So Competitive ..."

"Blessed is she who has believed that the Lord would fulfill his promises to her!"

Luke 1:45 NIV

It's that time of year again: our annual women's conference. Our small but mighty team is blowing up balloons, waiting for the Chick-fil-A to arrive, and finishing up last-minute touches. Our volunteer crew is firing on all cylinders as we prepare for nearly one thousand women, and I can't believe I've gone from dreading these events to truly enjoying every moment.

As I'm putting the finishing touches on the last few tables, one of our volunteers who always seems to be in the know comes and stands beside me like the cat that ate the canary.

"Hey there, you guys doing okay? Do you need my help with anything?"

Her eyes cut to the left and to the right before she closes them dramatically and takes a deep breath.

"You should know that a bunch of ladies won't be here tonight because they are going to another women's event down the street." She sighs a deep sigh that can only come from a woman who keeps a lot of secrets in her Patagonia vest, thankful to finally off-load one that she fears will bring me harm.

I feel my stomach tense up, knowing exactly which women and what event, but I don't give her the satisfaction of a reaction.

"I really appreciate you letting me know," I say as I rest my hand upon her shoulder. "We are really going to miss them, but God can be in both places. That's just one reason he is so awesome."

She stares at me as if I'm heartless, but it's beating heavy in my chest. I can feel the heat rising to my neck. I know this isn't a coincidence; for the last several weeks, other women in our ministry had told us the one woman was planning to intentionally host her event the same night as ours and I desperately want to believe my own words.

They will be missed.

God will be present in both places.

But deep down I really hope our event kicks the other event's butt.

The Race to the Front

At 7:00 a.m. every school morning, chaos erupts in my house. I'll hear it start upstairs as my two teenage daughters finish their makeup and hair routines, their socked feet pounding down the stairs as they grab their backpacks and shoes and then thunder down to the lower floor toward the garage. Without a hug or kiss or even a simple goodbye, throwing protein bars in their bags, they push like mini linebackers through the kitchen yelling, "I call the front seat!" over the top of one another, holding arms or purse straps in attempts to keep the other from getting ahead.

Some mornings one daughter will concede, and other mornings they draw blood as my husband sleepily starts the car, the radio drowning out their screams. I lock the door behind me, relishing the silence with a hot cup of coffee.

If you grew up with a sister like I did, you probably have scars that tell similar stories. I have one on my right arm where my sister took out a chunk with her nail because I won a board game.

Maybe you don't have a biological sister, but you spent years playing team sports where your teammates were like sisters, and you have reminders all over your body of games that got too rough. Or maybe you were part of a sorority or club and have emotional wounds—perhaps from fighting over the same guy—from words that were spoken about you that cut like a knife.

It is my belief that as young women we start our search for sacred sisterhood because we want to be part of something special. We want friendships that will pass the test of time and trials of life. I don't believe we enter every relationship or opportunity presented to us afraid we will be betrayed; rather, we optimistically enter, hopeful that we will find a lifetime of loyalty.

I also believe that as we age and mature in Christ, we look for other women who have already successfully navigated our current stage of life. We crave wisdom: from the moms who have already raised their kiddos, retired from jobs they held steadily for thirty-five years, or served faithfully in their church even in difficult seasons and circumstances. The hope is that God will use these women to help us navigate the murky waters of young adulthood and strange new seasons, and that they will see us as their collaborators, not their competition.

It is my prayer that my mentors see me as a co-laborer in Christ, not someone waiting to take their position in the Kingdom (as if that happens), and those I lead would see me as their greatest cheerleader.

But oftentimes these relationships get murky and the lines fuzzy when positions, status, and opportunities are up for grabs, and before we know it, we are acting like my two teenage daughters—fighting for the front seat of the car. What happens?

When a Paulette Becomes a Saulette

Okay, okay, I know these aren't real Bible names, but in keeping with the female theme of this book, stay with me. This is actually a thing.

Being a Christian woman is tough enough. So, when we find ourselves in a church or an organization where women are not just tolerated but celebrated, we know we have found something good and we don't want to let it go. When we find ourselves under healthy, women-led pastoral care and leadership, it feels like a gift from God—we can't wait to open it and share it with others.

In my early adult years of getting involved in church ministries, I preferred to work alongside men. Maybe this was a holdover from my familiarity with hanging out with a lot of guys in high school and college. But as I matured and my confidence in my identity in Christ grew, my ministry roles grew bigger and I was pleasantly surprised at how much I learned from women who were further along in their ministry journey. I looked forward to having these mentors in my life.

I longed for a sacred sisterhood among us that wouldn't compete with but contend for unity as the daughters of a house. After all, in the Bible, Timothy had Paul and that relationship fanned the flame from one generation to the next as the gospel of Jesus Christ was carried throughout the New Testament.

> **I longed for a sacred sisterhood among us that wouldn't compete with but contend for unity as the daughters of a house.**

Truth be told, most of the women I worked with on church staff and as a volunteer were in areas of ministry that held zero interest for me. As the worship pastor, I didn't connect with fellow women serving as the women's pastor or in the ministry (at the time) or the children's pastor. I was content in my part of the Kingdom but loved having my own "Paulettes" to cheer me on, women who were older than me and further along in their faith who challenged and championed me as we worked together for the same Kingdom purposes of loving God and his people.

There was so much ahead and so much to glean from others—what a gift that I didn't have to do it alone! But as I matured and grew in my anointing and authority, some—but not all—of my Paulettes grew antsy.

When I first began in women's ministry, the full-time women's pastor took it as her personal mission to mentor me as a teacher and preacher. For the first few years, everything was wonderful. She was an intimate part of my life and my family's life as I stepped into new arenas of ministry. I felt grateful for her expertise, wisdom, and connectedness to leadership to vouch for my hard work and growth as a leader.

But then, things started to shift. As I was given more responsibility, including things that had once been on her plate, and my visibility to the staff and congregation increased, she grew agitated. Where she once championed me, she now criticized me. Where she once encouraged me, she now told me what I couldn't and would never do. While she said, "I want to personally mentor you as a teacher," any time I was entrusted with something that was once hers, she created doubt in the same leadership to whom she once spoke of me with confidence.

I went from being a collaborator in the faith to a competitor in the field.

I wanted to run with the ministry God gave me, and I longed for a woman who would speak of me to others as Paul spoke of Timothy: "my true son in the faith" (1 Tim. 1:2). I dreamed of the time she would advocate for me again as a "true sister in the faith."

In her abuse, I longed for her approval.

I longed for guidance, as Paul provided Timothy: "You ... know what I teach, and how I live, and what my purpose in life is. You know my faith, my patience, my love, and my endurance" (2 Tim. 3:10). In other words, don't just say what I say, but do what I do.

I longed for collaboration like that between Paul and Timothy when he says, "Timothy, my fellow worker, sends you his greetings" (Rom. 16:21).

As I watched any hope of collaboration die away, she became more combative and I less trusting, until our meetings became calculated and contained no trace of mentorship.

What should I not say? Have I said too much? What could she use against me? How much of what she is saying is true?

I often think of the scripture in 1 Samuel 18:6–9 that tells of a similar scene between David and Saul.

> As they returned home, after David had killed the Philistine, the women poured out of all the villages of Israel singing and dancing, welcoming King Saul with tambourines, festive songs, and lutes. In playful frolic the women sang,
> Saul kills by the thousand,
> David by the ten thousand!
> This made Saul angry—very angry. He took it as a personal insult. He said, "They credit David with 'ten thousands' and me with only 'thousands.' Before you know it they'll be giving him the kingdom!" From that moment on, Saul kept his eye on David. (MSG)

Even though Saul had killed by the thousands and was still being mentioned in their song, he couldn't get past his jealousy and competitive drive to beat David.

From that moment on, Saul kept his eye on David ...

It sends a shiver down my spine!

Because that's what happened to my Paulette; she became a Saulette.

This confused many people who knew and loved her; she wasn't a bad person. She was funny and charismatic, witty and loving. She was a servant and true pastor at heart. As long as someone didn't pose a threat, they had nothing to worry about. It's important to know that someone's Paulette can be another's Saulette.

Eventually, Saulettes will fall on their own swords if they don't repent and get back on course. Because when our own agenda and personal kingdom building runs contrary to God's Kingdom plans or is at the expense of God's people, it will result in death. Death of a job, position, title, relationship, friendship, or mentorship.

This season of ministry taught me to be a bit suspicious of women who held authority over me in a working environment. Anytime we find ourselves under toxic leadership, it teaches us important lessons that can help us better lead others in the future. My prayer for women who find themselves in positions of power over other women is that we would:

- Lead with open hands and pure hearts.
- Receive God's grace to allow our ceilings to be the floor for the generation we lead.

- Invite women to sit at our tables, not to control them but to empower them.
- Mentor and disciple through biblical accountability and transparency.
- Equip other women to successfully run their race, even if we run in the same direction.

Eventually my Saulette moved to a position at another church. For so long I had been gaslit into believing all the criticism and tough "love" was for my own good, that her heart was to mentor and grow me in teaching and preaching, when it had been fear-based control.

It can be hard to identify a Saulette when we want to think the best of others and truly believe our Paulette is pure of heart. This is why it is important to have several women in our lives who can pray with us for discernment and offer wisdom. I had other trusted women in my life who also saw what I was walking out and were able to give me biblical advice on how to handle situations—when to wait and when to respond.

When details of what I endured under her leadership began to be revealed, there was complete shock from some who had only known her as the southern-aunt type who baked great bread and wore cool clothes. But for those like me who had been negatively impacted by her leadership over the last several years, there was a sense of relief that she couldn't hurt anyone again, and we could pray that she, too, moved on to learn and grow for the better in her next leadership role.

But those who remained were temporarily left asking: Could we ever thrive under the leadership of another woman, or were we forever scarred?

A Redeeming Paulette

When I lost my Saulette and I was left without any guidance in my new role, I can remember my senior pastor asking whom I would like to work under. After years of being in turmoil, I was tempted to ask for a male boss, which felt safe and familiar, as female leaders reminded me too much of her.

But I knew I needed a redemptive season.

There was an amazing female pastor on staff who was respected and loved, hardworking and intelligent. Everyone who worked for her was better after their time in her care, and I knew if I could have just a small season to learn from her, I could redeem what had been stolen from me in the form of trust and sisterhood. She was around the same age as my prior supervisor, and it felt like the Holy Spirit was offering me an opportunity for redemption, even though I was terrified to take the leap.

Working with her would mean being placed in her department and adding another job to my title, but I was willing to work extra hours if it meant I could heal. Before our first one-on-one, she asked me what I needed, and I was honest. I just needed clear communication, to be encouraged and challenged, to be held accountable and trusted. I didn't want ambiguous text messages at ten o'clock at night containing cryptic undertones that I was in trouble, or to feel as if everything I did was in direct competition with what she was doing.

As I risked making these requests known, I stepped into a new season with a true Paulette, and I was thrilled to find a sacred sister. I spent the next few years in her care unlearning toxic habits, sharing dreams, trusting feedback, and embracing her criticism as love, not because I was a threat. Meetings were something to look forward to, late-night texts when necessary were kind and invitational, and emails were direct and informative.

She taught me what it meant to be a leader who collaborated and created environments that fostered community. I was corrected, challenged, and changed by her leadership, and I am a better woman and friend because of her example.

Yes, women can compete with one another, but we don't have to destroy each other in the process of becoming stronger.

We can also be really good co-laborers who don't always see eye to eye but will always hold on to one another's hand.

What *you* carry for the Kingdom, dear sister, is not in competition with what God has entrusted to *me*.

Rewrite the Script

My sister and I are three years apart. (Yes, the same one who took a chunk of skin out of my arm for winning a board game.) As sisters we were as opposite as they come. She is blond and I'm brunette. She loves to cook and create beautiful cakes, and I use an air fryer like it's an Easy-Bake Oven from our childhood. She is attentive to details, and I fly by the seat of my pants (while still grabbing for control). She stands up for me in the comment section of my Instagram account when the trolls come out and I'm too passive to deal with them.

It's no secret there have been feelings of competition and comparison as two pastor's daughters with very different personalities, but we're also extremely close. We got married within three months of each other and got pregnant in the same month. When we found out we were pregnant at the same time, we were ecstatic. I can remember the day I found out I was pregnant; Hillary was already three weeks along and she was the first call I made to share the good news. Together, we hit a drive-thru for cheeseburgers and then we went to the store and picked out baby outfits so we could tell our mom together.

Our excitement for carrying new lives outweighed any sisterly competition from our pasts. Our daughters have grown up together, two very different young women with two very different mothers who are both deeply loved.

In Luke, we hear another story of two conceptions, one long awaited and the other a complete surprise. The two women weren't just friends; they were relatives.

In the beginning of this story, we meet Zachariah and his wife, Elizabeth, who were much older in age and had tried to have a baby without success. As this man is going about his priestly duties, an angel of the Lord shows up with a mind-blowing announcement.

"Don't fear, Zachariah. Your prayer has been heard. Elizabeth, your wife, will bear a son by you" (Luke 1:13 MSG).

Now you and I know this baby the angel speaks of would be John the Baptist, as the angel tells the soon-to-be-father of his coming child's purpose.

About six months into Elizabeth's pregnancy, the angel Gabriel shows up to a young woman named Mary, a virgin who just so happens to be the cousin of the newly-with-child Elizabeth. The angel explains to Mary that she, too, is with child in verses 29–33, saying,

"Mary, you have nothing to fear. God has a surprise for you: You will become pregnant and give birth to a son and call his name Jesus" (MSG).

Then, as if Mary isn't already reeling with this impossible information, the angel reveals,

"And did you know that your cousin Elizabeth conceived a son, old as she is? Everyone called her barren, and here she is six months pregnant! Nothing, you see, is impossible with God" (vv. 36–37 MSG).

To which Mary responds,

"Yes, I see it all now: I'm the Lord's maid, ready to serve. Let it be with me just as you say" (v. 38 MSG).

Mary doesn't waste any time. In fact, the Scriptures tell that she went straight to Zachariah's house and greeted Elizabeth. The moment Elizabeth heard Mary's voice, "the baby in her womb leaped" (v. 40 MSG).

The news of Elizabeth's pregnancy sent Mary on a journey so she could celebrate the miracle that was within her cousin. Being much younger and in a troubling cultural circumstance, when Mary received her overwhelming news, she ran straight to Elizabeth. I like to think it's because she was the first person Mary thought to tell and she felt comfortable processing what she had just learned with her. When she arrived, the baby within Elizabeth responded to the Holy Spirit who now dwelled within Mary. Even Elizabeth couldn't deny Mary was carrying someone special.

Special.

Not better.

Elizabeth broke out in song, singing,

> You're so blessed among women,
>   and the babe in your womb, also blessed!
> And why am I so blessed that
>   the mother of my Lord visits me?
> The moment the sound of your
>   greeting entered my ears,
> The babe in my womb
>   skipped like a lamb for sheer joy.
> Blessed woman, who believed what God said,
>   believed every word would come true!
>   (vv. 42–45 MSG)

To which Mary responded,

> I'm bursting with God-news;
>   I'm dancing the song of my Savior God.
> God took one good look at me, and look what happened—
>   I'm the most fortunate woman on earth!
> What God has done for me will never be forgotten,
>   the God whose very name is holy, set apart from all others.
> His mercy flows in wave after wave
>   on those who are in awe before him.
> He bared his arm and showed his strength,
>   scattered the bluffing braggarts.
> He knocked tyrants off their high horses,
>   pulled victims out of the mud.
> The starving poor sat down to a banquet;
>   the callous rich were left out in the cold.
> He embraced his chosen child, Israel;
>   he remembered and piled on the mercies, piled them high.
> It's exactly what he promised,
>   beginning with Abraham and right up to now.
>   (vv. 46–55 MSG)

They both carried a miracle. They both carried a son. One carried the Messiah and the other his holy harbinger.

Who Mary carried was not in competition with who was growing within Elizabeth, but rather in *collaboration* for all that was about to be fulfilled.

Elizabeth didn't accuse Mary of trying to steal her thunder. Instead, she prophesied over her cousin, bringing Mary comfort and confirmation.

Though the angel told Mary that Elizabeth was with child, Elizabeth had no knowledge of her cousin's condition. Yet when her baby leaped inside of her womb through the Holy Spirit, it brought revelation and encouragement *and* affirmation of what the angel spoke over Elizabeth's coming child in Luke 1:15: "he will be *filled with the Holy Spirit, even from his mother's womb*" (ESV).

Elizabeth models the tenderness and prophetic power we can exhibit in sacred sisterhood. When Mary enters her home, she:

- celebrates Mary and acknowledges what and whom she is carrying;
- welcomes Mary with humility and grace, honored she would come all that way to see her;
- speaks life over Mary and prophesies over what they both carried; and
- commends and encourages her faith.

Because of this gracious welcome, Mary, who had been on a long journey, responds with great strength and joy, singing a song of praise and exaltation.

What a joy to leave the house of a sister better than when we were first invited in.

When I feel panic rising, competition creeping ... when I start comparing my lot to that of my sisters, I will stop and declare these truths:

> What a joy to leave the house of a sister better than when we were first invited in.

- I am a child of the King. I am not stuck, nor am I forgotten.
- I am rooted and established in Christ, and he is sure of who and where I am.
- God is not finished with me yet; he has ordered each step I take to carry his Good News.
- God gives good gifts, and whatever he withholds is for my own good.
- God doesn't have favorite daughters.
- I will steward what I have been given.
- God has been and will be faithful to me.

We are not competitors climbing corporate ladders to be the first to break a glass ceiling.

We are cherished companions who each carry precious cargo for the Kingdom.

I see what you carry, and I call it blessed.

Flip Your Script

1. Is there a woman you see as your competition online, at work, in a friend group, or at church? How does this impact you spiritually as well as emotionally?

2. When you see another woman succeed, how does it make you feel?

3. When you succeed, how do you hope other women will respond?

Chapter 10

"Women Belong in the ..."

"By the grace of God I am what I am."
1 Corinthians 15:10

I'm meeting with one of our newest pastor wives in my office and she's scanning the walls, her eyes resting on my pastoral license certificate signed by our senior pastor.

"I love that they let women be pastors here."

I look up, surprised, so she continues. She shares her story and upbringing, telling me that where she comes from women aren't allowed to have the title of pastor, and even in her family the concept is taboo.

But she's so smart, smarter than me I conclude, as her vocabulary is extensive and intentional, her love of books and knowledge to be commended. I decide she is brilliant in the first ten minutes I am in her presence, and anyone who tries to hold her back is the dummy.

We spend an hour getting to know one another and I pray that once she settles, she will be one of the few pastor wives who frequents women's ministry. We need her calm, her steadiness, her thirst to learn more, her hunger for the Word of God. The more we talk, the more I want others to know her, and despite years of other people telling her who they think she is and where they think she belongs, she is strong and sure of who she is in Christ. I try not to act too desperate in my excitement as she exits my office.

It's important to keep an eye on the women the world tries to box in.

They have been known to break a glass ceiling or two ...

Cheers ⟩ Jeers

"Natalie, do you have any advice for how I should respond to this?"

I shielded the text message's glow in the dark movie theater, as a fellow female pastor, wife, and mom asked for advice on how to navigate yet another demeaning comment on her Instagram post telling her that, as a woman, she needed to stay home and take care of her kids rather than do the work of a man. One might assume this had come from a male, when in fact, it was coming from a fellow sister in Christ.

The cinematic music from the film boomed in my chest as I read the comment on her post over and over, my inner thespian crafting a mic-drop monologue to match the intensity of the score pumping through the theater speakers.

As someone who often posts on my social media platforms about my life in ministry as a wife and mom, I, too, have received

"Women Belong in the ..."

critical comments from women condemning me for choosing to work and sometimes travel. Whenever I post something for working moms, it's often met with criticism from one tribe of women and sighs of relief and freedom from the other. With time, I have learned to block and bless their hearts.

Recently I posted this to my social media account, not realizing the hornet's nest I was about to step into:

> For the working moms who have a ministry both inside and outside of the home: You were raised to believe it was the man who wins the bread, but you've always loved carbohydrates. You have an irreplaceable role in your home and hold daily residence in a corner office, behind a desk, in a classroom where you teach and walk church corridors where you preach.
>
> Don't worry about your children; God knew exactly how to wire them for a mother who would read them bedtime stories at night and run a company by day. They love you when you're with them and they are proud of you when you aren't. Your friends and loved ones watch you with admiration and they rise and call you blessed.
>
> God has given you the best of both worlds; He has gifted you with a calling that is unique and challenging, one that feels effortless on some days and overwhelming on others, but you won't

be consumed. He has given you everything you need to be a mother and an employee.

Don't apologize for your success—for loving a good suit and the quiet of your workplace after a morning of finishing late homework and packing haphazard lunches. Praise God for Google and Lunchables. Because when you come home your family is your ministry and you can serve from overflow, not leftovers.

It's not easy, you'll ebb and flow back and forth between wanting to stay home and wanting to conquer the world and there is plenty of time for both. God gives us seasons for a reason and He knows the desires of our heart; be honest about what you want and be what He wants. Our kids won't be collateral damage; God has them, and He has you.

Well done, you rare beauties who serve as CEO in the world and in the home. You build brands in one hand and a killer Lego house in the other and both make you special. Shake off the mom guilt and put on those stilettos—or whatever your shoe of preference—with confidence that God has ordered your steps and your home. What a beautiful life it is!

At first the comments were gracious and sweet.
"THIS. IS. WHAT. I. NEEDED."

"Thank you for this, it felt like receiving a warm hug from God and from other women who are living similar lives as mine."

"Weeping as I read this. Thank you for encouraging my weary, guilt-ridden heart."

Then the negative Nancys entered the party.

"Disagree on this one."

"I hate to say it, but I just feel like being a mama should be the main focus for a ministry."

"You are out of line; a woman's most important role is her family."

I wasn't upset that people disagreed with the post. What shocked me was the back-and-forth debate among women as they fought to defend their position as a working mom or stay-at-home mom, or hybrid of the two. It was like a screaming match between those who loved their careers and children and those who believed a woman could only truly leave a legacy within the four walls of her home. Both sides of the coin brought very valid points, and yet nothing was truly accomplished.

The point of the post wasn't to convince stay-at-home moms to enter the workforce or working moms to quit to raise their families. It was meant to encourage a group of weary women looking to find others who could relate and encourage them in a very demanding season.

The end result was working moms made to feel guilty for their success and some stay-at-home moms feeling devalued by the "boss babes" who believed they lived a lavish life of watching soap operas and hosting playdates at the local Starbucks over lattes.

The post itself failed every test, and I had hoped we would just pass one: It appeared that women had a difficult time cheering one another on in seasons we either could not understand or refused to empathize with due to our personal beliefs and convictions.

And that is what made me saddest of all. As women, especially Christian women, we were more concerned about our opinions than one another. We couldn't see past our own reflections to stare into the heart and soul of a sister who didn't need our criticism but our compassion, even if we couldn't relate.

The comment section could have been a cheering section.

Instead, it was a jeering section.

Working Girls

I've had a job since I was old enough to get a work permit. As a pastor's kid who came from a family where my parents were bi-vocational out of necessity, and who worked hard and with excellence, working wasn't optional. Trust me, most of my jobs haven't been passion projects or sources of interest, but rather whatever I could find to pay the bills in that season.

At fourteen years old, I began work as a restaurant hostess. I progressed to a waitress, where I would be covered in farm-style au gratin potatoes and chocolate cake before making my way to a babysitting job or a friend's house for a girls' night. I didn't grow up with a trust fund; if I wanted gas for my car, food, or spending money, it would be earned behind the steel counter of a commercial kitchen and from the generosity of customers I truly enjoyed serving—most of the time.

I went to college on a series of grants and work-study programs that required me to work a certain number of hours on campus, so I shelved books at the university library. Upon graduation, I went right into the school system where I taught classes by day and aerobics on the weekends. I watched as many of my girlfriends graduated college with marketing and education degrees only to get married a year or two later and never step foot in a boardroom or a classroom. I can remember having coffee with my single girlfriends and they would say, "Looks like she just paid a heavy tuition to get her MRS degree ..." and we all laughed out of a twinge of jealousy.

Not too long after their "I do," I would receive a baby shower invitation. I showed up as the single friend in my work clothes, gift in hand, as they sat in front of a fireplace in a home so grand it felt like we were little girls playing dress-up.

I had attended the same college as these women and hung out with the same crowds, but our lives began to look like two completely different movies set in the same hometown with alternate endings.

As social media was just coming of age, it became easier and easier to stay in touch with my friends, but also peer into the living rooms and baby showers, wedding photos, extravagant vacations, or stay-at-home-mom routines of perfect strangers. Now I wasn't just comparing my life to the lives of women I actually knew, but to those whom I had never and would never meet.

In all the chaos of being single and working fifty-hour weeks, never once was I compelled to drop into the comment sections of these elaborate, seemingly humble bragging posts and say anything to make another woman feel guilty, inadequate, or less than because her life looked different than mine. Did I have to block a few of them? Did I need to put some boundaries in place to not get sucked into the comparison trap? Sure! But over time, as I stepped into my future day by day, I found confidence in what I was good at, who I was reaching, and the life God had so generously given me.

When we as women say things like, *"Looks like she just went to college to get her MRS degree ..."* and *"maybe you should focus on your children more than your job ..."* it is saying more about us than those we are actually speaking about and to.

Decoding Girl Talk

I have become fluent in interpreting girl talk and the underlying messages we convey without actually saying them. I have learned that emotions, difficult seasons, trials, exhaustion, hormones, anxiety, our relationship with our husbands, issues with our children, all the unchecked boxes on our to-do list, and so many other things drive much of the outward conversation from our inner dialogue, which is informed by our own past traumas, experiences, and expectations in life. Whew!

We feel justified in our justice, projecting our childhood and young adult realities onto others with their own understandings of the only world they have known, and then judge success or failure based off very biased views.

Just as I couldn't expect my friends to understand what it was like to be raised in a pastor's home, I didn't know what it was like for them to grow up in a home where money was always there, but their dad was always absent.

As adults, we worry that what happened to our mom or dad will happen to us, that their story is destined to be ours. Often, we don't realize we're shouting the same regurgitated scripts over our lives when we have the power to make them look very different than that of our parents or upbringing.

We can focus so much on what other women have been given, what other women get to do, or how they look, that we lose focus on what God has created us to do.

> We have the power to make the scripts over our lives look very different than that of our parents or upbringing.

So, we say things about other girls and women to make us feel better and convince ourselves we are satisfied, when in reality we are screaming for things to work out for us just once—as they seemingly do for our sisters in Christ.

My oldest daughter plays high school volleyball, and she recently went to a camp where she spent a few days with some of the best athletes in our state. At 5'5", she wasn't the tallest and couldn't jump the highest, but she was a powerful player and a valuable asset. Standing among her peers, some over six feet tall with impressive collegiate vertical jumps and pending scholarships, she suddenly felt insecure as a teammate.

After a frustrating day of working on a few challenging skills, my normally calm, levelheaded girl just exploded, her face red, eyes brimming with tears. She began analyzing her teammates as if they were competitors and her own body as if it were her enemy.

"The only reason they are so good is because they are so tall. If I was that tall, I could block all the balls too ..."

I let her go on for a few minutes before going into full-on mom mode.

"You listen to me right now. Never once has your height been a concern—you have never allowed your size to stop you from being a consistent player, good teammate, and amazing athlete. You spent one weekend with girls who are older, taller, confident, beautiful, and suddenly you're insecure? If you want it, you work for it, and if you work for it, the work will pay off. But don't ever underestimate or devalue what you have been seeking all this time: to be a good friend, a witness to those who don't know Jesus, and a light to those who live in darkness. If you seek that out, all the other stuff will fall into place, 5'5" or 6'5"."

I reminded her of what Jesus says in Matthew 6:33, to "seek the Kingdom of God above all else, and live righteously, and he will give you everything you need."

When we seek him first, he works all things out for his glory and our good, faithful to finish everything he starts in us and through us. Not because *we* are good or deserving, but because *he* is good and deserving and will use us—temper tantrums and all—to accomplish Kingdom work.

So, when we say things like, "Well, if I looked like her, I could get a boyfriend too," or "No wonder she got that job or role—look at her!" we are implying that what we carry or who we are is not enough, and that God isn't capable of opening doors on our behalf simply because we weren't created with the same hair color, body size, bank account, or family tree.

Our speech betrays us over and over. Not until we learn that what we are really saying comes from a place of deep insecurity and fear are we able to decode the words spoken over us by our fellow sisters that cut down rather than build up.

When my friend asked me what she should do about the comment left by a fellow Christ-following sister who chose to tear down rather than build up, I remembered something a pastor once told me as my own social media following was growing and the trolls were showing up. He said, "Natalie, let those who know and love you defend you." So, I did what so many other sacred sisters have done for me, and I made my way to that comment section.

Rather than condemn the woman who had ignorantly chosen to say hurtful things that only brought shame, I simply rewrote her comment, but changed all the negatives to positives, to demonstrate that it's possible to have differing opinions on where a woman might have the most impact while also supporting decisions that need to be made due to different life circumstances.

Whether we break glass ceilings in stilettos, change dirty diapers, run a company, or run a household, every woman has a unique calling and gift set that gives her authority wherever she has been entrusted to lead.

Women work hard every single day in many different capacities, none greater than the other, but unique in title, position, and season of life.

The only way to change the way we speak about our sisters is to change the way we speak about ourselves.

A Balancing Act

As a wife and mom who travels all over the world, one of the main questions I am asked is, "How do you juggle ministry and motherhood?" I don't have a scripted answer for this because sometimes I'm not juggling it; sometimes it feels like I'm dropping lots of balls, but my kids know they are the one ball I won't drop.

As women, we often find ourselves not just surviving but thriving in the struggle. We were made for this—for wearing different hats and juggling lots of balls in the air. So, when we find ourselves either choosing to work a traditional job, sit on the school board, join a committee, or step into areas of leadership, finding other women who can champion us is a gift.

As we learn to walk this tightrope, we find comfort knowing there is a safety net to catch us should we fall, in the form of community and friendship. Knowing we have the support of other women, both younger and older, who will stay strong in our success and failures along the way gives us a security to walk into rooms with the confidence to accomplish the most challenging of tasks. But this takes women secure in their own identity in Christ to lift us up over their own desires.

> **Knowing we have the support of other women, both younger and older, gives us a security to accomplish the most challenging of tasks.**

When my girls were little, we had kids in our home all the time while their parents worked late—from the neighborhood and the church. Sure, they got dinosaur-shaped nuggets and French fries for dinner rather than their moms' gourmet pot roast, but at least they were safe and had fun.

When my kids travel with me now and we find ourselves in another state with friends or family, they are sleeping on couches and running errands with other families while I'm at book signings or my husband is driving me place to place.

I never worry that my kids aren't being loved or taken care of because the family of God, especially my sisters, have always been a second home for us. Yes, I'm their mother and they prefer my presence, but God has given them a giant Kingdom family that stands in the gap in my absence.

Whether we are in the workplace nine to five, a traveling nurse, a teacher, a pastor, a doctor, a lawyer, or in our homes tending to our spouses and children, women need each other. It won't always look like it did in school or in our twenties with girls' trips to exotic locations or nights out in sparkly dresses and heels. As time goes on, it will look like walking a sister through a divorce, the loss of a child, a big move, a job transition, depression, or difficult teens.

It might look like sitting next to a sister during her chemo treatments, ringing the bell when she finishes her last radiation appointment, cleaning her house before a big event, dropping off a meal when you know she's had a long week, or sending her a digital Starbucks gift card so she can sit in silence with a good book over a hot cup of coffee because school just started and she is desperate for some peace.

Sacred sisterhood is celebrating the wins, sitting in the sorrow of losses, and speaking life over situations or circumstances—even in comment sections of social media posts—because we truly care about each other's families, ministries, and lives.

It's being so confident in who we are and whose we are that jealousy, envy, strife, and injustice can't outrun our love for one another.

Rewrite the Script

My freshman year of college, I started to attend a women's Bible study where we dove into the desirable attributes of a godly woman. Several of the young women had mothers who stayed home with them most of their lives, and it seemed these girls had similar aspirations. They unapologetically wanted to be wives to godly men, have babies, and stay home with their families as long as possible.

I found this to be a noble option, but as someone whose mom modeled to my sister and me how to hold a job both inside and outside of the home, yet still attended all my school functions, it never occurred to me that my life would be any different. I planned on using my degree and working even after I had children, but there weren't many Bible studies for young women like me.

I remember feeling guilty some days as I left our small group, wondering why I couldn't seem to figure out this Proverbs 31 woman described as:

"Her clothes are well-made and elegant, and she always faces tomorrow with a smile" (v. 25 MSG).

"When she speaks she has something worthwhile to say, and she always says it kindly" (v. 26 MSG).

"She keeps an eye on everyone in her household, and keeps them all busy and productive" (v. 27 MSG).

The word "meek" kept coming up over and over again in our group discussions. I thought being meek meant never using my voice, never having an opinion, and losing who God made me to be to appease a man who might take me as his wife. I came to the startling conclusion I would most likely be single forever because

I wasn't elegant, I didn't always think out my words, and I didn't want to keep my household busy 24/7.

Then I learned about Esther, a beautiful queen who was given the opportunity to save her people, and her *meekness* brought a revolution.

In her ability to operate with power under control, she went to the king and asked for her people to be spared. She prayed, she fasted, and she brought other women into her plan by asking them to pray with her. Only then did she use her God-given voice to contend for something bigger than herself. It could have cost her life had she asked too soon, too late, or reacted out of emotion rather than power under control.

Being meek didn't mean I can't use my voice.

Meekness meant I knew how and when to use my voice, even if it meant with power and authority to bring change for the Kingdom and possibly even freedom for those in bondage.

Take a look at this list, sister, of the Proverbs 31 woman:

- She is trustworthy.
- She is generous.
- She is financially responsible.
- She is creative.
- She is spontaneous.
- She likes the morning.
- She enjoys fixing meals for her family.
- She plans her day.
- She's an entrepreneur.
- She is a hard worker.

- She knows what she is worth.
- She is skilled in things in the home and outside of the home.
- She is a servant.
- She gets her family ready for all seasons.
- She likes to wear colorful clothing.
- She buys and sells what she makes.

The Proverbs 31 woman is a lot more than we have made her out to be.

She is you and me.

It doesn't matter the level of volume we speak at, how much we talk or don't talk, how much we like crowds or want to be alone; God will use us to bring order and beauty to our homes and the lives around us as we are obedient to love him and others. There isn't a cookie-cutter Christian woman like some creepy Christian Stepford Wife. We are all uniquely made by the Father to accomplish the work he has set at our hands, and it will take all kinds of personalities to bring lost sheep home.

It doesn't matter where our fellow sisters or brothers believe we belong if God has given us keys and access to a particular position or platform. What he has for us, nobody can take, and being a woman doesn't disqualify us from Kingdom work. He didn't forget and accidentally make us women. He was intentional in making us and is so very proud of our tenacity, conviction, and passion to deliver the Good News everywhere we go.

Be encouraged in this: "God has given each of you a gift from his great variety of spiritual gifts. Use them well to serve one another. Do you have the gift of speaking? Then speak as though God himself were speaking through you. Do you have the gift of helping others? Do it with all the strength and energy that God supplies. Then everything you do will bring glory to God through Jesus Christ. All glory and power to him forever and ever! Amen" (1 Peter 4:10–11).

Flip Your Script

1. How has the enemy used your current stage of life to make you feel guilty or less than compared to other women?

2. What are you personally struggling with about this stage of life? Maybe you're a new mom, starting a job, a newlywed, single for the first time in a long time, living on your own, a widow, an empty nester. What is hard? Where do you see God?

3. What is the one thing you wanted to do or become when you were a little girl? Dream with her again and ask God to remind you of those things that brought you to life. Writing, music, art, building a business ... Just because a season is new doesn't mean God has forgotten the dreams of your past. He isn't finished with you yet!

Chapter 11

Golden Girls

*"Make new friends, but keep the old;
those are silver, these are gold."*

Joseph Parry

If you would have told me five years ago that I'd be a women's pastor, I would have rebuked you and told you to keep that prophecy to yourself. But here I am, four and a half years into doing some of the richest and most profound ministry of my life and about to tell my team that it's time for me to pass the baton.

All my journaling in the early days of my associate women's pastor role had turned into a social media account where I started talking about why I wanted to quit but why I was going to choose to hold on, and a ministry called Raised to Stay had been born. For the past five years I have been encouraging my tiny Instagram account. It has exploded overnight and I now have a book releasing next summer and speaking engagements lined up for the next year. Over the past few weeks, my husband and I have been praying for direction; and the moment we felt God release me from full-time ministry, we knew my team would need to be the first to know.

Two of these amazing women have been with me from day one of taking the full-time women's pastorate, and in a plot twist, I also hired the pastor's wife who blew me out of the water just a few months back. We're sitting in my office like we do every week, and I can see on their faces they know what is coming. It has been apparent for some time now to anyone who knows me well; my assignment is complete.

Before I open my mouth, their tears are flowing, and now mine are too. What used to be sobs of, "God, let me quit," are now sobs of gratitude as I give final speeches and take a moment to personally speak words of life and affirmation over each of them. They have been my prayer partners and greatest confidantes, hard workers and humble servants, true sisters in the faith who champion me and trust me. In this moment, all I can do is pray I've done the same for them.

They promise to keep running and I tell them they are going to change lives for the Kingdom, and I mean it with my whole heart. I didn't want women's ministry. I would have never chosen it, but God chose it for me.

He didn't need me to pastor his daughters.

He needed his daughters to pastor me.

Silver and Gold

I spent summers around campfires as a Girl Scout singing these words penned by a poet from the 1800s who seemed to know a bit more about friendship than my ten-year-old brain could comprehend. *"Make new friends but keep the old; one is silver and the other gold."* The melody was catchy and comforting, familiar to us all after years of repetition and tradition. As I looked across the warm embers at my fellow Troop 1174 members, some digging their sticks into the ashes and others squirming to reposition themselves on the log beneath them, I knew enough to know I was lucky.

I wanted to bottle up each and every one of them just as they were and protect everything that made us who we were in that exact moment. Awkward, obnoxious, innocent, goofy, safe ...

Eventually we outgrew our colorful patches and friendship bracelets. Junior high and high school came in like a freight train along with hormones, boyfriends, athletics, school dances, and all the drama of being teenage girls. Some of us handled it with grace and others of us went kicking and screaming, holding tightly to our safety blankets and each other.

I'll never forget when, in the fall of my senior year in high school, my best friend and I walked over to her house across from the high school to change into our cheerleading uniforms before our home Friday night football game. Once we were all dressed in our kelly-green-and-white paraphernalia and bows perfectly in place, we sat on her floor with an hour to kill. We had spent years in her bedroom playing everything from Barbies to Mall Madness, our favorite board game. We even played bank with an old cash register her mom had found us, including expired checks and rogue Monopoly money.

I can remember feeling so big in that moment as I surveyed her walls covered in dance trophies, pageant crowns, and cheer flags from our last twelve years. I looked over to see her on her belly underneath her daybed, grunting as she pushed past old stuffed animals and shoes, squirming out from under the iron frame holding a relic, our old cash register. With a ding, she pressed open the cash drawer and the Monopoly money was in place just as it had been when we last opened it, the checks stacked, some written on in our newly developed third-grade cursive.

For an hour we giggled as we wrote large checks for a new Porsche and handed out hundreds to each other for a trip to the spa. For a moment, time stood still, and we were just two little girls playing in an alternate world, but then reality set in. Suddenly, we were both very aware we were two eighteen-year-old cheerleaders playing bank, and with one awkward push of the cash register back under the bed, we jumped to our feet and thundered down the steps to make our way toward the field. We never spoke of it again.

Fool's Gold

While many of us know the first part of Mr. Parry's poem, like many of our friendships in life, we don't often get past the first few lines. Life has this cruel way of setting us around campfires singing "Kumbaya" only to leave us with the cold ashes of memories of friendships we thought were forever but had an expiration date. One of the greatest fears of mine was being forced to move away from my friends and start over at a new school in a new city or state. Nowadays, this is normal life; we expect for people to leave and move on, and we are expected to welcome in those new to our communities. Being the "new kid" is no longer taboo; rather, it is the norm.

And nothing tells you the worth of the gold in your friendship like moving away.

When my youngest daughter was ten, we moved from Colorado back to our hometown in Kentucky. We had lived in Colorado for nearly seven years; she was leaving behind her besties, and I could tell she was doing her best to be brave and believe she would establish strong friendships in her new school.

While my older daughter and I heard less and less from our Colorado friends, Selah's crew was constantly calling her phone and even mine to FaceTime and connect on Messenger. She gave them tours of our new home, carried the phone with her around our yard letting them meet our new kitten, and they played with their toys with their phones propped up so they could see each other. They just wanted to be together.

The girls are all teenagers now and still squeal in delight when they get to see each other in person, picking up right where they left off as if no time has passed. At a young age they understood that what they had was real gold, old friends who started living life together at four years old and who I believe will still love each other at forty.

> It takes a long time to make old friends.

It takes a long time to make old friends.

The truth is, not everyone who starts with us will end with us, and while some were taught to embrace friendship as covenant, others learned not to get too attached because finding a lifetime best friend was as rare as finding real gold.

Many thought they had found the real deal only to discover it was fool's gold, and rather than continue sifting through the soot for the real thing, they stopped searching for sacred sisterhood altogether.

But even within the disappointment of counterfeit connections and pseudo sisterhood life has brought my way, I still believe the real thing is worth searching for, fighting for, defending, protecting.

Joseph Parry continues his poem:

> *New-made friendships, like new wine,*
> *age will mellow and refine.*
> *Friendships that have stood the test—*
> *Time and change—are surely best;*
> *Brow may wrinkle, hair grow gray;*
> *Friendship never knows decay.*
> *For 'mid old friends, tried and true,*
> *Once more we our youth renew.*
> *But old friends, alas! may die;*
> *New friends must their place supply.*
> *Cherish friendship in your breast—*
> *New is good, but old is best;*
> *Make new friends, but keep the old;*
> *Those are silver, these are gold.*

When you look back to your childhood, who are some of those old friends that were true gold in your life? The beauty of social media is that we can find almost anyone—maybe there's an old friend worth digging up. It does a heart good to sit down over a cup of coffee or a playdate to reminisce about times and places only the two of you can recall.

Nostalgia might just be a healing balm for a few of our lonely hearts.

Gold Digging

It's no secret that finding and nurturing sacred sisterhood takes time. It takes commitment through seasons and transitions over the course of adulthood, and few of our childhood friendships survive the long winter of those early adult years.

When my Paulette turned Saulette and was no longer mentoring me, I realized I had very few safe women in my life who I could call to ask for advice or for prayer. There were always my friends back home who were in similar phases of life, with elementary-aged schoolchildren, all hanging on for their lives. But calling them with work problems felt like I would be a burden and, if I was honest, I didn't feel like explaining my new work situation.

However, there were two or three amazing women who had opened their office doors to me on days this new assignment felt as if it might crush me. They weren't the obvious friend choice; I was forty and they were in their fifties and sixties.

But I knew if I was going to survive this season of ministry, I needed to do some gold digging.

I needed to make some old friends, and quickly.

That meant new levels of vulnerability and trust as it was earned, availability on my part to not just lean on these new sisters, but for them to trust they could lean on me. I was going to need more than one Paulette in my life, and she couldn't be imitation gold. I needed the real deal.

As I began my new assignment in women's ministry, these women showed up to every event, gave me feedback, and prayed over me constantly. They came over to my new house and anointed it with oil—shoot, even anointed the dog—and wrote verses in secret places that I would uncover from time to time just when I needed them. They celebrated my children's birthdays, came over for the holidays, and they quickly became like family to us all.

My husband would see me struggling with a decision or worried over a meeting and ask me if I had called them for advice. He knew they were a lifeline at a time I felt as if I were drowning. There were late-night phone calls where I was sobbing uncontrollably, early morning coffee meetings in our pj's in my living room, and deliverance prayer sessions behind closed doors as we warred for unity in our church and ministries.

Turns out, I didn't have to dig too deep or too long; God is the best with connecting his daughters for Kingdom purpose. All I had to do was express a need and desire for friendship, comradery, company. Sacred sisterhood chips away at our hardened hearts to expose a golden center under all that tough exterior.

When the time came for me to take over the entire women's ministry, I knew it was going to come with a lot of scrutiny from the women who hadn't quite warmed up to me as their new women's pastor. I also knew I would need an entire team around me of other pastors and leadership who would help me develop a ministry that wouldn't just bring a bunch of women into a room for a social hour, but train them up as leaders, teachers, and true sisters in the faith. This would take time and creating something I myself had fought for a long time.

It felt so ironic that the one thing I said I'd never do was now my main role at the church and in the Kingdom. God was going to teach me one way or another a very important lesson:

God loves his daughters, and he wants us to love one another.

For the next several months, the very women's ministry I said I didn't want became a safe haven of women drawn to the mission and vision God had given my team and me as we worked hard to bring unity to not just the women of our church, but our staff.

Women weren't a script to write for, a group to be defined by colors or activity, but rather an army of God's daughters ready for war, in season and out of season. We would train, equip, and empower through the Word of God and encounter with the Holy Spirit so each of them knew they had a voice, a vote, and a veto when it came to leadership and their role in the ministry.

> **The very women's ministry I said I didn't want became a safe haven of women drawn to the unifying mission God had given us.**

I went from hiding from these women to seeking them out. From running from this assignment to embracing it. From counting the days until it was over to knowing my days could be numbered, so I needed to maximize every moment I was given to ensure each woman was set up for success.

Turns out, when you dig for gold, you get a treasure chest.

How quickly those silver stars turn to gold in the hands of a good Father.

Silver and Gold

These spiritual big sisters and mamas in the faith who weren't family by blood but who helped raise me up are the real MVPs. Since I was a little girl, my parents allowed trusted women leaders in the church to invest in me with wise counsel and spiritual direction. When I got to public university, the first thing I did was find a campus ministry and begin exploring mentorship and discipleship under female leaders on campus. I knew how far some of the women of our churches had carried me through my teen years, and I figured it was safe to assume my college years would come with their own drama.

These older women, or "golden girls," found me when I needed a voice of reason to speak into my life and provided extra hands to help carry me over the finish line. They relayed the same messages my parents and pastors had been trying to get into my head but with a different method because they knew how I worked and what motivated me, what discouraged me. To this day they bring the late-night phone calls, lengthy text threads, coffee meetings that turn into conference calls, and come-to-Jesus moments. They calm my hot tempers and cool my hot tears.

These golden girls help us grow, develop, mature in Christ, and sit beside us as spiritual midwives to deliver the dream, the calling, the thing deep inside of us that seems too big and impossible. They point us to Jesus, call us higher, and put us in our place when we get arrogant or whiny.

They are the voice of reason with a heart of platinum, opening their homes, their lives, their families to make room for us. They take risks on a stranger because they know there is a great reward on the other side. These women are heaven sent and hell's threat as they parent a generation into our God-given assignments. They go before us as generals in the faith with a protection, and it's easy to honor where they have been as they prepare us for where we're going.

In my early twenties, I may have been ungrateful and seemingly uninterested, grabbing the batons of the saints before I had learned how to run a clean race, but these women have been my greatest cheerleaders, and today I am their biggest fan.

I love how Paul references Timothy's mother and grandmother who raised him in the faith, saying, "I remember your genuine faith, for you share the faith that first filled your grandmother Lois and your mother, Eunice. And I know that same faith continues strong in you" (2 Tim. 1:5). Timothy, raised by two golden girls, finds a mentor in Paul who carries on with training him up in Christ. Paul encourages Timothy, saying, "You've been a good apprentice to me, a part of my teaching, my manner of life, direction, faith, steadiness, love, patience, troubles, sufferings" (2 Tim. 3:10 MSG).

Timothy was part of Paul's everyday life, and because he had good examples in his mother and grandmother, he knew what to look for in someone who would lead him as he went about ministry.

As Christian women, we need other women who have been where we are going and who did it well. We should be willing to do the same for the generation behind us. We are often referred to the Proverbs 31 woman, and there is much to learn from her, but I'm also interested in being a Titus 2 woman. Paul describes how a woman who is beyond childbearing age can invest in the lives of younger women. I like this list of attributes the Titus 2 woman carries:

> Similarly, teach the older women to live in a way that honors God. They must not slander others or be heavy drinkers. Instead, they should teach others what is good. These older women must train the younger women to love their husbands and their children, to live wisely and be pure, to work in their homes, to do good, and to be submissive to their husbands. (vv. 3–5)

Now, before you freak out and assume I'm insinuating that we should all be mentored by a woman who will demand we be stay-at-home moms and work for our husbands, hear me out. The Titus 2 woman:

- Uses her words to build up.
- Teaches good things.
- Mentors younger women.

- Is purehearted.
- Works hard.

Whether single, married, with children, or without, all women can relate to the Titus 2 woman or would benefit from knowing a Titus 2 woman. She is a golden girl. She is our first phone call after a difficult meeting, our first FaceTime when we need prayer for a situation, our first text message when something good happens. She has been where we are and can see a mile away any land mines or traps that might be set for us as we blindly navigate new jobs, relationships, motherhood, ministry, and life in general.

She could be an old family friend, someone you meet at church, a leader or pastor, a neighbor. We can have more than one at a time, and they might give varying opinions and suggestions, but the common denominator is a deep love for you and desire to see you flourish.

> We need other women who have been where we are going and who did it well. We should be willing to do the same for the generation behind us.

Many of us have had a Saulette who didn't model the Titus 2 woman very well. So, when we found our Paulette, we didn't want to let them go. Some of the most amazing golden girls we allow into our lives will be friends, people we've known our whole lives who know what we are going to do before we do it.

Not all golden girls are older women. Sometimes, it's the sister from another mister of the same age who has seen your good, the bad, and the ugly and loves you too much to let you act like a fool. She may not be older and wiser, but she is feisty and ferociously loyal to protecting and championing you in the big and small.

And when you find her, don't let her go.

Rewrite the Script

In 2023, after nearly seven years of living over a thousand miles from my hometown, we moved back to be closer to family. Raised to Stay was taking me around the world and we longed for our girls to grow up with their grandparents, aunts and uncles, and cousins. I didn't know what to expect. I knew the girls would make friends quickly between school activities and youth group, but would the friends from my past want to be friends with the me of the present?

As word traveled that we were back, my phone began to light up with text messages and phone calls from familiar area codes, comforting voices on the other end that had matured over the years but were still recognizable. Plans were set: lunch dates, afternoon matinees, evening walks. There was so much to catch up on and I worried too much time had passed for us to act as if no time had passed at all.

What we have to understand about sacred sisterhood is that we can put it on the shelf and surround it with pillows donning cross-stitched sayings, but it's always there for us. We can disclaim it and deny it, but time cannot compete with the love between God's daughters who were created for sisterhood.

With each gathering, we picked up right where we left off, reminiscing about high school and asking if we'd talked to so-and-so. We sat in restaurants on hot summer days showing each other pictures of our kids on our phones and tearing up over how they had grown overnight, and before we knew it, three hours had passed like three minutes, the backs of our sweaty thighs stuck to the patent leather booths.

When I looked back at our time in Colorado, not just my friendships but the friendships my daughters had formed in such a short amount of time, I realized how blessed we were to have friendships made of silver and gold.

We made new friends.

But we made sure to keep the old.

And what we get is buried treasure filled with so much beauty, history, stories, and laughter that when we're tempted to believe all the scripts we've been taught to read over each other, we can write our own.

Of giggling women in their forties recalling their early twenties and stupid decisions they made.

Of mourning sisters in their fifties when a spouse passes away far too soon.

Of empty nesters, learning how to golf for the first time to take their minds off missing their babies and breaking a car window because they were that bad.

Of coworkers who are having a hard time navigating a new system or boss and who lean on each other to get through each day.

Of new next-door neighbors, neither of whom can cook, but who have morning coffees from their decks as their children run amok below.

Of women of faith, who welcome the lonely and marginalized in sacred sanctuaries from the church to the home who will never have to say, "I don't even like women," because they have been so loved by those who have come before.

Do you see the value of the treasure we hold?

Invaluable.

Irreplaceable.

Cherished.

Nonreturnable.

Nonrefundable.

Sisters, you might have started out a piece of coal. But there's a diamond at the core.

May we never stop digging for the treasure that lies within each of us.

Flip Your Script

1. Who were your closest friends when you were a child? What made them special?

2. Who are your closest friends now? What makes them unique? How are you a good friend to them?

3. If I'm honest, question 2 is hard for me these days, so I'm asking myself this and inviting you to the journey ... "Who are the old friends I miss and would love to reconnect with online or in person, and who are a few women I respect and admire that I'd love to get to know in this stage of life?" Today sounds like a good day to reach out and find some silver and gold.

Chapter 12

My Sister's Keeper

*"Your people will be my people,
and your God will be my God."*

Ruth 1:16

I'm on the front row surrounded by women, some of my best friends to my left and to my right. I resigned from my role as full-time women's pastor three months ago in the middle of planning our huge spring women's conference and told the team I didn't expect to speak since I would no longer be their pastor.

The new women's pastor—yes, that wide-eyed sister who sat in my office in awe that a woman could even have the title "pastor"—called me and insisted I stay on the speaker lineup, and I don't think I've ever felt so honored before. My final assignment before our family moved back to our hometown in Kentucky is preaching to the women who taught me how to love women and to the team that ran with me the entire way.

The room is filled now; worship is coming to an end and my time to speak is nearly here. Their new women's pastor takes the stage as we sit, and I wonder how I will be introduced. After all, no matter how well-planned, transitions rarely go without a little awkwardness.

The room grows silent, and she begins to speak. "This morning, we have the privilege of hearing from Pastor Natalie, who has been women's pastor here for the last four and a half years. God recently called her and her family out to full-time ministry on the road, and it's an honor to have her here with us. Can we all stand and thank Pastor Natalie for her years of pastoring us and pouring into us?"

The room is now filled wall to wall as women have trickled in during worship. I am at a loss for words as the women around me begin to stand, clapping and whistling and cheering as I sit with tears pouring down my face.

Their new pastor is now smiling at their former pastor, and I think we are all the most blessed women in the world to have a Father who would love us all so much to teach us how to model the beauty of sacred sisterhood.

And he sees what he has asked us to carry, knowing its worth and giving us each other, our sister's keeper, to make sure the enemy can't steal the precious cargo within us.

You Are Priceless

You can imagine with all the treasure we carry as women how valuable we must be to the Kingdom of God and what a threat we are to the powers of darkness. The enemy wants nothing more than to kill, steal, and destroy everything we represent and offer this world in the form of hope and love.

Women, we can change nations and bring others with us into the Kingdom of God, and that terrifies our enemy.

Whether it is a time of joy or a season of grief that brings us together, God is intentional in how he aligns his daughters for both sacred sisterhood and Kingdom mission.

Many years ago, a woman and her family made the difficult decision to uproot from everyone and everything they knew and move to another city where they were strangers. For ten years they established a new life, the husband found a job, and the sons married two lovely women with hopes of growing their own family. But tragically, the woman lost her husband, and then the unthinkable, she lost both of her sons. This woman was now widowed, childless, and had nobody to protect her—nothing to her name.

Knowing she had little to offer her daughters-in-law (too old to find another husband), she did her best to encourage them to go back to their homes and start over, to remarry and make families of their own. As she sent them off with blessings and deep gratitude for the love they had shown her and her sons, she knew the moment they were gone she would truly be alone.

But she wasn't prepared for what happened next. As one wept goodbye and began her journey back to her home, the other was reluctant to go. The woman began to plead with her daughter-in-law, telling her to follow the other, who was well on her way back to her family and everything she had once known. Yet, she couldn't be persuaded to leave her mother-in-law's side.

Instead, she doubled down on her decision to stay right where she was, and the woman knew it was a battle she couldn't win. So, the two women, unified by great loss and grief, lived their lives in an uncommon friendship marked by a shared experience of death that could have robbed them of life, but instead gave them family.

Though it could have been written about any woman who has had great loss in recent years, this ancient story of Naomi and Ruth gives us a front-row view of life as a woman in Israel in 1100 BC and the unique roles and challenges many of us can identify with as women today. Not much changes under the sun, even thousands of years later.

The recipe for this friendship wasn't nostalgia, girls' trips, wine, coffee dates. It wasn't based off proximity, success, wealth, goals, or season of life. This sacred sisterhood was forged through pain, discomfort, sacrifice, commitment, mutual respect, and loyalty—but above all, love.

In Ruth 1:15, Naomi tells Ruth, "Look ... your sister-in-law has gone back to her people and to her gods. You should do the same."

She sees what her life is going to become and doesn't want Ruth to be weighed down by an old woman without a purpose or plan.

But Ruth sees beyond what Naomi can do for her or give her and responds:

> "Don't ask me to leave you and turn back.
> Wherever you go, I will go; wherever you live,

I will live. Your people will be my people, and your God will be my God. Wherever you die, I will die, and there I will be buried. May the LORD punish me severely if I allow anything but death to separate us!" When Naomi saw that Ruth was determined to go with her, she said nothing more. (vv. 16–18)

In a world where the life of young women depended on men, Ruth chose to align herself with a sacred sister.

The Secret Sauce to Sisterhood

If we were to combine all the ingredients of this relationship between Ruth and Naomi, we would find a very good start to the secret sauce of sisterhood.

- They were loyal to one another and God.
- They allowed their friendship to be tested by trials.
- They sacrificed their own wants and desires for what was best for the other.
- Naomi led Ruth as the older generation.
- Ruth trusted Naomi in her old age and honored her.
- They had an unconditional love for one another and for God.

What if Ruth had allowed all the things she had heard about mothers-in-law and women affect her decision to stay with Naomi?

What if she allowed all their past disagreements to make her bitter?

What if she had been embarrassed to be seen with an old woman without status or title?

What if Naomi had been proud and refused to let someone younger help in her time of grief?

What if Naomi had harbored resentment toward Ruth for things that happened during her marriage with her son?

Because both women were willing to love the other more than they loved themselves, they saw God working all things out for their good and his glory. The story of their friendship has been studied and inspired women for generations as an example of what happens when we view our ordinary lives and friendship as extraordinary for God. The friendships he gives us aren't just for our convenience but so he can unite his daughters in seasons of joy and sorrow, celebration and grief, life and death—to make their Father's name known to others looking for family.

Sacred sisterhood beckons to come find a seat at God's table and take part in a Kingdom inheritance that cannot be taken away. It creates an unbreakable bond that the enemy knows has the strength to defeat him simply in the unity of the daughters of God.

Don't Mess with the Sisterhood

My oldest daughter was verbally bullied by her volleyball teammate who wasn't getting any playing time. Because Annabelle was starting in this other young lady's position, she found herself the butt of her jokes, snide remarks, and backhanded compliments. She hoped the intimidation would cause her to start making mistakes and, in turn, get her spot back.

My husband and I coached Annabelle as best we could, knowing these life lessons would one day be valuable as she came up against other insecure mean girls. She wasn't her enemy—there was something deeply broken in this teammate to have her identity so wrapped up in volleyball that she couldn't see how much Annabelle really valued her as a friend.

But the other teammates began to take notice and heard the things being said, watching as Annabelle stayed quiet and kept her head in the game and not the drama. Without her asking for it or even knowing it, an upper-class teammate went to the coaches on her behalf and told them of all the harassment and unnecessary behaviors taking place behind the coaches' backs. Annabelle was called into the head coach's office the next morning, there was a team meeting, and by bedtime Annabelle was receiving text messages from her team telling her how proud of her they were for treating this girl with such kindness following several weeks of torture.

And that teammate who had gone out on a limb on her behalf? She was a sister's keeper.

Though the hurting teammate would continue to make things a bit awkward for my daughter throughout the rest of the season, this one girl couldn't compete with the sacred sisterhood that had formed between Annabelle and a few others on the team. Would they be best friends for life? That's still to be determined.

But for the moment, they were a small, strong army who protected their own in a sea of mean girls and gossip girls.

Sisters fight for each other, not with each other.

Sisters protect each other; they don't target one another.

Sisters defend each other; they don't leave the other out to fend for themselves.

And perhaps it is the bonding over a bully that has haunted them or a bad volleyball game or failing the same test that unifies them for a time.

Sacred sisterhood ensures that we won't have to do it alone.

We Belong to Each Other

If we take all the things we say about each other as women, and all the scripts culture writes for us that they just assume we will adopt, we will see a common thread.

As humans, not just as women, we often allow our own insecurities and sin to keep us from truly loving one another as Christ loves us.

> **Naomi and Ruth honored each other's sacrifice rather than be jealous of one another.**

Difficulty united Naomi and Ruth when many of us are looking for everything to be easy and drama-free.

Conflict strengthened Naomi and Ruth when many of us will cancel one another rather than work toward healing and reconciliation.

Naomi and Ruth honored each other's sacrifice rather than be jealous of one another.

Ruth told Naomi she would go wherever she went, and Naomi's God would be her God, when so many times we simply stop praying or sitting in the unknown because it's uncomfortable or mysterious.

God used Ruth's loyalty to Naomi to do even greater things than what we see in the initial story. Their friendship would see God's promises fulfilled further down the line, one of a Redeemer who would come and crush the power of sin and death.

Our sacred sisterhood has the potential to partner with the promises of God for our generation and generations to come. The God of Ruth is our God today, and our very own friendships can introduce other women walking as weary wanderers in their grief and loneliness to their very own Kinsman Redeemer, the One who delivers and rescues.

The Ministry of Women

Those four and a half years I spent in women's ministry changed my life and taught me that as this generation of women attending and serving in the local church, we have the opportunity to rewrite the script and introduce the ministry of women to our girls in a new and fresh way.

Women's ministry today doesn't have to be exclusive, boring, or focused on crafts and weird little sandwiches. It can be a transformative space where women form lifetime bonds and forever friendship.

Women can rewrite our reputations from gossips to intercessors.
Women can go from emotionally charged to Spirit-filled.
Women can be known for how we love one another.
Women can stop fighting for microphones and start warring for our sister's prodigal. Her healing? Her deliverance? Her calling?

I see her; I can hear the war drums behind me as the women of God begin taking their places in the church. Some of us whisper and some of us roar, but our voices touch heaven and shake hell.

> **Women's ministry can be a transformative space where women form lifetime bonds and forever friendship.**

We have an opportunity to flip the script, to go from crafts and tea parties to prayer meetings and revival. You won't want to lead it; you'll fight it and say you don't like women, but God loves his daughters, and he will teach you to love them as well.

Lead them.

Love them.

Fight for them.

We are the very feminine heart of God, and our intercession, our unity, our anointing reaches the throne of our Father.

The church needs women's ministry for these five reasons:

- **Community:** Creating community, not just a program, where every woman has a seat at the table that invites the Holy Spirit and fosters unity. A healthy culture will expose the lie of competition and the trap of comparison that naturally develops among isolated women at a young age.

- **Collaboration:** A shared platform opens doors for women of all ages and interests to feel included and valued. Should a leader or volunteer move on, there are several others equipped and championed to step into areas of leadership.

- **Conversation:** Creating space for dialogue in small groups rather than just creating another church service provides a holy place for women to lead one another. You don't need a celebrity or huge personality to lead your women's ministry; rather, several women dedicated to listening and loving each other well.

- **Reinforcing Core Values:** Women's ministry shouldn't be the source, but rather a resource of the local church. By pointing women to the core values and mission of their local church, we give them opportunities to partner with, not compete with, initiatives already in place to worship, connect, and serve beside their families and one another.

- **Multi-generational Ministry:** When the women of God serve the women of God, multiple generations are impacted as we preach the gospel, meet needs, and fulfill the Great Commission. Generational curses can be broken, and generational blessings established and called forth.

Rewrite the Script

Now that I am far removed from all the emotion that came with stepping into women's ministry, I can take personal inventory of what was lacking in me, not only as a woman but as a child of God. It's never easy to look into our souls and ask God to search us and convict us of where we have fallen short and sinned.

From an organizational standpoint, the process of my job description being radically changed and how leadership went about it wasn't perfect, but God allowed it.

I blamed the pastors and those responsible for the change, but God had a plan.

When I honestly look at my own behavior in the flesh and my beliefs of who God was in that season, it is clear that there was work that needed to be done and a ministry that would be produced as good fruit if I was willing to be pruned.

Sure, I went kicking and screaming, but God knows how to step over us and let us yell it out before we finally fall asleep from exhaustion and surrender to his ways.

I was also terrified I wasn't qualified to lead hundreds of women, many who were nearly double my age. What did I have to offer these saints who had already raised their children and were now raising great-grandchildren, when my own were barely out of elementary school?

Yet, even in my insecurities and reservations, I knew there were Ruths and Naomis in the room.

Marys and Elizabeths.

Esthers.

Deborahs.

Lydias.

I decided if the Lord was truly asking me to shepherd this group of women, no matter how long the assignment might be, that I would literally work myself out of a job. I would equip them and encourage them to lead with all their strength, but it would take training and practice and confidence to move from spectator to active participant in the ministry.

One by one we saw their confidence increase, their leadership expand, their tables grow, and before we knew it, they were launching their own small groups, taking meals to one another when a baby was born or someone was sick, and partnering with other groups to visit prisons and nursing homes. We watched the Great Commission go out before our very eyes.

We were an army.

My heart had broken for the women God entrusted to me, and I went from screaming at my boss, "I don't even like women!" to standing before them on a Tuesday night weeping as I said goodbye and looked them each in the eyes and said, "I love you," meaning it to my very core.

Because you fight for sacred sisterhood.

We contend to be our sister's keeper.

It doesn't come naturally, but it is written into our DNA as daughters of the Creator.

It would be godly women who healed my perception of women.

It would be the older generation who patiently watched me fumble my way through leadership, their prayers carrying me when I was still keeping them at an arm's distance.

It would be the younger generation who cheered me on and showed up to support me as we were getting started, when I was still kicking and screaming my way into the room.

And to this day, when I go back to visit and stand in the back of the room as now hundreds of women gather weekly for community, worship, and time in the Word of God, tears still stream down my face because it was this place and these women who showed me the beauty and power of sacred sisterhood.

They rewrote the script for me, line by line, chapter by chapter, as they loved me when I wasn't even sure I liked them. They followed me when I didn't know where I was going because they trusted our God. They prayed for me when I didn't know how to pray for them. They cheered me on when I didn't even want to be in the game. They believed in me when I was too broken-down to believe in myself.

And when it got difficult, when there were some women who were still trying to bring in dirt from old gardens, they stood beside me.

There are women who will stand beside you too.

We just have to give each other a chance and so much grace.

May this be the year you find sacred sisterhood and rewrite your script from, "I don't even like women ..." to "I am my sister's keeper."

That is a book worth reading and a movie worth watching.

Sacred sisters,

I love you.

And I really like you.

Epilogue

I have journals dating back to my junior high school days. I poured my heart out to the Lord in them begging him to make a way for my mom to homeschool me. I felt left out, lonely, and insecure and pleaded with God for real friendship with just one girl my age.

Every few years I pull those journals out to revisit the scripts I recorded in my perfected cursive handwriting in classrooms, the lunchroom, the gymnasium, and after dances. Middle school Natalie wanted so much to be part of something special, to experience those friendships I saw modeled on my favorite Friday night teen sitcoms that promised an adolescence with a built-in bestie and a boyfriend—set to a musical montage.

Yet my real-life script was messy and unedited, much like the journals I continued to fill through high school, college, marriage, and having babies with a familiar heart cry: I don't want to do any of this alone.

This topic of friendship and sacred sisterhood has been one I've wrestled with privately since I was just trying to find a seat in the cafeteria. But now this book feels like the all-school assembly in *Mean Girls* where we're gathered in the bleachers acknowledging we've all been personally victimized by the Regina Georges of the world.

And we've all been someone's Regina George.

As an author, through my books I want you to feel like you're getting a sneak peek into my box of journals, a front-row seat to a life that has been full but not perfect. My hope is in these pages you find another human who has been where you have been, maybe even where you are now, and for just a moment you can take a deep breath and rest that you aren't alone.

As a Christian author, my hope is that we aren't stuck sitting in those bleachers trauma bonding over rejection and isolation, but that my words point us all to Jesus and his heart for his daughters. I pray I have given you some courage to box up all your journals from the past and start writing new scripts for your own lives—as well as the lives of your daughters and granddaughters.

Often, when we finish books that inspire reflection and a resulting desire for life change, we ask ourselves, *Now what?* There's an expectation of next steps or action on our part to execute some of the principles taught. When I've shared with women during the writing of this book, there has been overwhelming support for this topic. So I want to leave you with a few things we can do as women, especially Christian women, to help us find biblical, sacred sisterhood that will bring joy to our Father and to those we meet.

Rewrite the Script

Get a new journal and start fresh! Write out your prayers asking God for the type of friendship you desire. Do you need a Ruth or Naomi? Maybe a Mary or Elizabeth. Perhaps a Lois or Eunice, a spiritual mother or grandmother. Ask God to bring her into your life at church, through others, or perhaps you already have someone in mind. Be specific: God already knows the desire of your heart.

Put Your Feet to Your Faith

Is there an old friend you haven't spoken to in years? Maybe you had a falling-out and miss her, but don't know how to reconnect? Take the first step and send a message, a text, an email. Tell her you've been thinking about her and would love to talk on the phone or meet for coffee. If God has placed someone on your heart, no matter how many years have passed, pick up the phone or stop by her house and step out in faith. It may not go how you want it to go, but at least you'll know you tried, and you can either close that chapter or possibly open a new one.

Be What You Need and What You Want

Go out of your way to serve the women in your life. Model what it looks like to love unconditionally, to serve without asking for anything in return, to show up when others won't. Send that text message with a Bible passage and word of encouragement, send the flowers, the gift card, offer to watch her baby while she sleeps for the first time in weeks. Be the friend, the mentor, the sacred sister you are praying for to someone else and watch God begin to bring those sisters into your path.

Don't Grow Weary

Finally, remember it takes a long time to make old friends. We may not be at cafeteria tables anymore, but those old scripts die hard. Be patient with yourself and with others. As women, we all have things that hang us up and hold us back, but we need each other, and we are worth fighting for. You are worth fighting for. Keep trusting and believing God has women he will bring into your life who will remind you that *you actually do like women ...*

Natalie

Notes

1. Mara Wilson, *Where Am I Now? True Stories of Girlhood and Accidental Fame* (New York: Penguin Books, 2016), 196.

2. "Jane Austen Quotes," accessed May 13, 2025, www.janeausten.org/jane-austen-quotes.php.

3. Melissa Harrison, "Stop Creating Drama, You're Not Shakespeare," *Melissa Harrison M.S. Master's Level Life Coach* (blog), March 3, 2021, https://melissacatherineharrison.com/stop-creating-drama-youre-not-shakespeare/.

4. Sharon Hodde Miller, "Women, Insecurity, and the Self-Help Gospel," TGC, October 4, 2017, www.thegospelcoalition.org/article/women-insecurity-and-the-self-help-gospel/.

5. Sean Covey, *The 7 Habits of Highly Effective Teens: The Ultimate Teenage Success Guide* (New York: Simon & Schuster, 2011), 201.

6. Naomi Torres-Mackie, "Gender and Jealousy: The Dangers of the 'She's Just Jealous' Consolation," *Psychology Today*, June 6, 2019, www.psychologytoday.com/us/blog/underdog-psychology/201906/gender-and-jealousy.

7. Zayda Slabbekoorn, "15 Emotional 'Inside Out 2' Quotes That Are Deeply Meaningful to Anyone Struggling Right Now," Your Tango, June 19, 2024, www.yourtango.com/quotes/emotional-inside-out-2-quotes-meaningful-anyone-struggling.

8. Tia Ghose, "Mean Girls: Women Evolved to Be Catty?" LiveScience, October 27, 2013, www.livescience.com/40717-indirect-aggression-between-females-works.html.

GOD CAN HEAL CHURCH HURT

Raised to Stay provides healing and hope to those hurt by church people. Written by a pastor's daughter, Natalie Runion has firsthand experience with the painful wounds of church hurt. Her personal healing journey, combined with encouraging biblical advice, will help you passionately pursue Christ and persevere in your calling.

Available everywhere books are sold

DAVID C COOK
transforming lives together

150 YEARS STRONG

DAVID C COOK

JOIN US.
SPREAD THE GOSPEL.
CHANGE THE WORLD.

We believe in equipping the local church with Christ-centered resources that empower believers, even in the most challenging places on earth.

We trust that God is *always* at work, in the power of Jesus and the presence of the Holy Spirit, inviting people into relationship with Him.

We are committed to spreading the gospel throughout the world—across villages, cities, and nations. We trust that the Word of God will transform lives and communities by bringing light to the darkness.

As a global ministry with a 150-year legacy, David C Cook is dedicated to this mission. Each time you purchase a resource or donate, you're supporting a ministry—helping spread the gospel, disciple believers, and raise up leaders in some of the world's most underserved regions.

Your support fuels this mission.
Your partnership sends the gospel where it's needed most.

Discover more. Be the difference.
Visit DavidCCook.org/Donate